ACCOUNTING

PRINCIPLES

The Ultimate Beginner's Guide to Accounting

Table of Contents

Introduction

Accounting is meant to communicate information, both inside and outside of a business. Think about the amount of confusion that would be caused if companies devised their own methods of reporting? How could stock investors decide to invest or banks determine if a company was worthwhile of a loan without an accurate, clear accounting method that offered a snapshot of a business entity's financial health?

Accounting principles are those generally accepted rules of accounting that everyone agrees to follow. This provides transparency and clarity in financial reports. In addition to being critical for reporting information about financials, proper accounting helps companies find problems and solutions and encourage growth through their company.

Do not worry if you are unfamiliar with accounting—the first chapter will break down some of the basics and terms you need to know before you get started. From there, we'll move onto the elements of accounting, including the Generally Accepted Accounting Principles (GAAP) of the United States and show you how to apply these principles to real-life accounting scenarios. You'll find detailed descriptions and examples that should make understanding the application of these principles easier. Finally, you'll find additional detailed rules as issued by the Accounting Principles Board and the Financial Accounting Standards Board. These will also need to be applied when doing accounting.

While the idea of learning accounting can be intimidating, this book will break it down in a way that makes things easy. It is perfect for:

- Business executives who want to read financial reports

- Business owners and CEOs

- Financial analysists

- Stock market investors

- Marketing experts

- Taxpayers

- The average person

There are plenty of reasons to learn accounting. The field of accounting can help people in all levels of business to analyze and understand financial reports. This information can be used to spot potential problems in the business and decide how to best allocate revenue. Looking over accounting details can also provide valuable information for marketing your company or expanding your business. It also helps provide insight into how to best manage taxes at that time.

In addition to benefiting businesses, learning the basic principles of accounting can benefit the average person and taxpayer. People who closely monitor their finances are more likely to be prepared in the event of emergencies. They have a clearer picture of their incoming funds, their expenses, and how much they need to save. This lets people experienced in accounting have better control over their lives.

Now that you know some of the benefits of accounting and why you may want to learn it, it's time to dive in. Best of luck!

CHAPTER 1

An Introduction to Accounting Principles and Important Terminology

Before we dive right in, this chapter will provide you some context. Before you start reviewing accounting principles, you'll need to be clear on the vocabulary used and some of the most basic accounting fundamentals. Don't worry if you aren't there yet—this chapter will provide the necessary background information to help you understand the rest of the book.

What are Accounting Principles?

Accounting principles are those regulations set as they are needed to create more cohesive accounting techniques. Regulations generally build over time. As regulators find the need for new accounting principles to be implemented, they are introduced. However, as the need for regulations determines which regulations are put into place, not all accounting principles are the same. The principles of accounting discussed in this book will be the generally accepted accounting principles (GAAP) of the United States. While this book may teach the fundamentals of accounting, you'll want to learn the rules and regulations in other countries before conducting business there. Even though there is an International Accounting Standards Board (IASB) that exists at the global level, there is not yet a set of accounting principles accepted worldwide.

In the United States, you'll find that there are three elements of accounting principles. The first is the basic rules and guidelines. By understanding these basic principles, you can have a scope of what is expected when reporting financials. The second part of accounting principles is general industry practices, which are the way that the accounting guidelines should be applied to real accounting practices. Finally, consideration must be given to the detailed rules that have been issued by authorities including the Accounting Principles Board (APB) and Financial Accounting Standards Board (FASB).

Why Are Accounting Principles Important?

Without set guidelines, the field of accounting wouldn't be as worthwhile to people outside of the company that may not understand a company's reporting techniques. Accounting is a system and principles govern that system. Accounting encompasses all things related to the systematic recording, reporting, and analysis of the financial standings and transactions of a business. It is necessary for analyzing how well a company is performing financially and it allows investors to consider factors like the overall net profit of a company.

Developing a Conceptual Framework for Accounting Principles

Even though many accountants believe there would be a benefit to a specific set of rules for accounting, particular in those situations where judgment is needed and the way to report financial information is not always clear, there has yet to be a specific set of rules. The principles discussed so far in this book have been based on those ideas set forth according to generally accepted accounting principles. These generally accepted principles make up a rule-based method, as companies that do not adhere to the rules may be audited, face fines, or face other consequences. However, the principles discussed are only part of the equation. In the United States, there is also a Federal Accounting Standards Board, which is considered the foundation of appropriate accounting processes. You see, the phrase 'generally accepted accounting principles' actually has three sets of rules. The first set of rules cover the principles and guidelines we have already discussed in this book. The second part of these guidelines is the detailed standards rules set forth by FASB. Finally, businesses and accountants should also take care to report using the generally accepted industry practices.

This can be confusing. As a result, all publicly-traded companies must have an external certified public accountant to review their financial statements. This independent auditing process ensures that companies do not skew the information themselves to reflect better and attract more investors. In this chapter, we'll talk about the FASB and their role in accounting.

Principle-Based Accounting vs. Rules-Based Accounting

One of the challenges that many accountants face is being diligent in staying current with reporting methods, as well as making decisions about how to handle the financial transactions of a business. In a way, the GAAP guidelines are a system of rules that should be used. However, some companies may struggle with applying the rules to their specific businesses. This is one of the reasons its so important to understand how to apply the principles—it is not just enough to know them and hope for the best. Accountants should also conduct research when they are unsure, as failing to report something properly can have a serious impact on the financial statements of the company. It can also result in a risk of auditing, fines, and even jail time if the offense is severe.

To maintain the principle of consistency, it is not uncommon for businesses and accountants to keep their own rules handy when completing financial statements. This might include information about the preferred method of depreciation, how to value the inventory, and other guidelines that must be followed to remain consistent. This ensures that regardless of which employees are helping compile the financial statement, the information is going to remain the same.

The best guideline for accountants who are unsure to follow, aside from doing research, is to always back conclusions using the appropriate calculations and analyses of the financial information. This is especially true in cases where it may not be as clear how to best handle the accounts.

FASB: The Importance of Developing a Framework

With the wiggle room allowable under current laws, it is no surprise that a framework was practically demanded. The biggest struggle accountants face when applying the principles of accounting is formally identifying these principles to follow them. The rules of accounting are based on concepts rather than specific laws, however, there are real consequences for those who do not follow them.

The problem is that it would be nearly impossible to develop a set of rules that could govern every situation in accounting. This is the reason there are options for reporting events like depreciation. Even so, it is important that accountants follow their best guidelines when reporting financial information, whether it is information shared by people across the stock market or information for the IRS.

You can think of the principles of accounting as a settled basis and framework. Authorities have agreed on these principles of accounting and the way they have been used. One of the struggles, however, is finding a framework that is established around the world. Though there is an International Accounting Standards Board, they have not agreed upon a set of principles that can be used worldwide for accounting. For this reason, it can be difficult to compile and analyze financial statements from other countries.

A Brief History of United States Accounting Principles

In the world of finance, the call-to-action in creating a standard for accounting is considered one of the major markers of the 20th century. Many organizations, individuals, and committees developed over time in an effort to create an authoritative basis for accounting. However, many of these rules, standards, principles, concepts, conventions, and guidelines failed, simply because they did not capture the full conceptual framework for what organizations were trying to achieve by developing a set of standards.

As organizations and individuals continued in their efforts, two distinct schools of thought evolved regarding the field of accounting. The first school of thought held the core belief that accounting principles did not require a systematic theoretical foundation. Many believed that the principles should be learned through practice, even though this could have serious consequences and would make it harder for new accountants to practice proper accounting. This school of thought also supported the idea with a few basic guidelines, accountants would be able to solve any problem they encountered during accounting practice. One major contributor to this idea was George O. May, one of the most influential accountants during his lifetime. He agreed with this first school of thought, even referring to accounting principles as a 'distillation of experience,' an idea that he mentioned in the title of his book published in 1943, *Financial Accounting: A Distillation of Experienced.*

Even though these earlier ideas about not needing a framework and relying only on the practice of some of the more practical rules regarding accounting were popular at the time, accounting matured, business practices became more complex, and the idea of establishing a generally acceptable set of terms for accounting was revisited once again. Even so, that represented an important time for accountants and practice. Those accountants that were able to use their knowledge of accounting practices often specialized in certain fields, which made accounting a rather limited field. As with many other areas where the idea of learning on the job was practiced, it was eventually learned that it was not enough for accountants to specialize in one area. Without having a direction for the knowledge learned in those fields, the world was no closer to establishing an accepted set of accounting principles than it was before.

The earliest idea of an accounting principle can be traced back to a committee known as the American Institute of Accountants. This group was chaired by famous accountant George O. May and worked to determine a specific role or function for people who worked as accountants. The Special Committee on Co-operation with Stock Exchanges met to work with other accountants and audit the various financial records of publicly-traded companies at the time. The committee assembled following the rapid stock market decline of 1929. The depression that followed left many people looking for somewhere to blame and accountants were there as the scapegoat, as it was believed that erroneous and inconsistent accounting principles were to blame. After reviewing the list, the group believed that there were too many accounting methods being used to develop a fair, consistent way to evaluate the various companies. As a result, the committee decided to clarify the responsibilities of accountants and auditors, educate the public about accounting and its limitation, and establish a way to make financial statements more accurate and informative.

The efforts of the committee were helped along by the New York Stock Exchange, which also had vested interested in improving the way publicly traded entities disclosed their financial information. The report consisted of a series of letters between the Exchange and the Institute, detailing various transactions and analyzing their effectiveness. The letters were exchanged between 1932 and 1934. They were titled *Audits of Corporate*

Accounts and became a major factor in the establishment of accounting principles, being republished in 1963.

It was in these letters that they discussed the idea of accepted principles of accounting. A group of lawyers, accountants, and corporate officials came together and decided there should be a framework for accounting principles. If a corporation reported its financial information within those set guidelines, it would be considered acceptable. For this to work effectively, however, it was also agreed that companies must disclose the methods they used in reporting. The methods chosen also should be applied consistently, which would allow an accurate portrayal of the changes in a company's finances from period to period. Even though the generally accepted accounting practices had not yet been agreed upon or put into writing, two ideas had already been established. The first was the idea that companies should use consistent reporting methods for an accurate overview of the financial standings of their company. The second was the idea that companies should disclose their methods so that auditors, stakeholders, and the general public had a full picture of their finances. The committee believed that companies would be more likely to act and report ethically since they now had to maintain transparency in their transactions.

The Earliest 'Principles'

Even though the committee was far from establishing the generally accepted accounting principles that we know today, there were several rules discussed in a very important letter dated September 22, 1932, and sent from the Institute committee to the New York Stock Exchange. In the letter, they described the general idea that the value of an asset (their description used a plant) should be matched against gross profits through the entire life of the asset, which would give a better portrayal of where revenue was being generated. They also mentioned that it was commonly accepted to state inventories at the lower value of either the total cost of manufacturing or sourcing the item or the market value of the item. In addition to these guidelines found within the text of the letter, five principles were listed. Here is a summary of each:

1. Companies cannot realize a profit by crediting it to an income account until it has been earned. Profits should remain unrealized until the service is fulfilled, as the amount does not affect the ordinary course of business otherwise. It was recognized that profits should match the expenditures and outflow that was used to generate those principles.

2. Paid-in capital and capital surplus should not be used to generate income while being listed in the dividends area. If a company relieves the income, it can cause problems when stockholders try to collect on their accounts. This may have been one of the contributing factors to the stock market crash since stockholders were pressured to withdraw their funds as the economy lowered and many companies saw the costs of their

stocks depreciate. Corporations lost funds because of this, particularly those that had realized this capital as part of their income.

3. This rule basically stated that corporations must be their own entities. Even if there is retained earnings or a surplus of net income, this cannot be used to fund the actions of a child company or parent company. Two companies that exist mutually under the same owner cannot do business together, as this would be unethical. They also cannot share funds.

4. Treasury stock can be realized as an asset within a company, however, it cannot be disclosed as a credit to the income. Rather, treasury stock must be realized as part of the comprehensive income of the statement and kept separately.

5. Companies must classify their notes or accounts receivable, as failing to classify can leave confusion about a company's debts. As some are related to financing activities and others are related to operating activities, a company's finances would be misconstrued if these activities were grouped together.

Even though these early rules were the closest to developing a standard of accounting, they still did not have the fundamental, comprehensive, and timeless qualities that many people were looking for at the time. This made it hard to have them established as principles, as they were not concrete enough. Additionally, the committee had identified exceptions in nearly all of the cases, which made it hard to agree that there was an application for those five rules across all areas of accounting.

Challenging the Committee's Rules

Another notable document was published in 1937, this one a contest run by the Institute. A man named Gilbert R. Byrne wrote an essay that won first place in the contest, titled "To What Extent Can the Practice of Accounting Be Reduced to Rules and Standards?" In his essay, Byrne stated the problem was that the committee misunderstood the distinction between a principle and established terms like procedure, convention, and rule. The ideas presented were closer to rules than principles and they did not serve as fundamental principles since the ideas were more about auditing techniques or how things must be presented on financial statements.

Byrne also discussed the dictionary definition of principle, mentioning that he believed the committee had erred in the way that they considered a principle. Rules and policies can be laid down, but it is harder to establish a principle. It can be declared, but not established, as principles are outside of any committee or single individual's governing rule. Principles can be used to help establish rules, but a principle must be considered as a general truth before it is applicable. Once it has been declared as a general truth, even then the principles need to be interpreted and applied differently depending on the specific circumstances.

Furthermore, Byrne and others at the time believed the Institute committee had failed in setting the principles because they required accountants to adhere to something that had not been established yet. It was a heavily criticized system and it ultimately failed. However, it still provided that basis of a conceptual framework and helped those who criticized the system better clarify what exactly an accounting principle was and how it could be declared. After being challenged, the committee still failed what it set out to do. They had all but given up on the idea that there could be any fundamental set of core principles applied to the field of accounting and it was concluded it would be a waste of tie to continue trying to identify and state these principles.

George O. May finally took to his books and started defending the idea of principles, noting the committee's definition of a principle as it was established: "A general law or rule adopted or professed as a guide to action; a settled ground or basis of conduct or practice. According to this definition, the committee had been much closer to establishing principles than they had realized. He also argued that it would be nearly impossible to establish these principles, as they were few in number and would have to be written in a general manner to apply to a wide range of accounting scenarios. In this regard, May was correct. The generally accepted accounting principles used today offer broad definitions that can be applied to a wide range of scenarios.

Following all these arguments, it was finally agreed that the major focus would be in creating transparent and consistent statements. Within each organization, there would be a clarified section of laws or rules that should be followed when creating documents. If the companies were forced to disclose their methods, anything that was unethical or unwarranted would incite public outcry. To maintain a publicly-traded status, corporations would also be subject to regular auditing. Each corporation that was listed in the New York Stock Exchange would have to prove to an auditor that their code consisted of generally accepted principles to maintain its listing and continue receiving the benefits of being a publicly traded company.

The Securities Act and the Securities Exchange Commission

In 1934, the Securities Exchange Act brought the Securities and Exchange Commission into existence with the hopes that they could regulate the accounting practices of the time and establish guidelines that everyone could follow. Like the Institute committee, the SEC was concerned about the many practices used by companies (and approved by auditors) for listing on the New York Stock Exchange. The Chief Accountant of the SEC met with other important figures and the Institute in 1937 and stated that steps must be taken to reduce the differences in accounting practices. Otherwise, the SEC would be forced to step in and produce rules that accountants must follow, regardless of practices. For corporations to be allowed to continue operating, the committee would have to issue a series of statements that had 'substantial authoritative support'. This substantial support would be from experts in the accounting field and other authorities who would also analyze the stated principles for application and practice across all areas of accounting.

The original plan was to issue a comprehensive statement that would include all the accounting principles that accountants would need to follow when reporting financial information. However, the process of identifying and stating these principles was lengthy. It took almost two decades for some of the principles to be established. Rather than waiting for an entire list, the committee decided to state principles as they were discovered, hoping that it would buy them more time.

Other Contributors to Financial Standards

Though the committee had failed to create a comprehensive list of principles, two other groups of the time each established their own idea of financial standards and generally accepted principles. One of these documents was titled "A Tentative Statement of Accounting Principles Underlying Corporate Financial Statements". This was composed in 1936 by the Executive Committee of the American Accounting Association. The consistency idea was presented in their work, but it was also noted that there should be a consistent accounting framework that could be used. The association emphasized that the best solution was identifying and strengthening a framework that could be realistically applied to various areas of accounting.

On the completely opposite end of the spectrum was a paper published by two professors of accounting and a professor of law, Thomas Henry Shanders, Henry Rand Hatfield, and Underhill Moore. Their paper on accounting theory was called *A Statement of Accounting Principles* and was published in 1938. In the document, they compile a variety of discussions, surveys, and interviews with accountants currently practicing and results of some of their practices. It emphasized the idea that there was no underlying systematic or foundational theories in place and that the current system was working. Additionally, the paper emphasized that an accountant's duty was to know when to take it upon themselves to report in accordance with their experience and when to defer to the company's management for further instruction. It was only through asking questions that further guidance could be received, as there were no principles established at the time. Though it did not necessarily establish any set principles, this paper was most noted for its analysis of current practices and the thorough nature of research. Additionally, through reading the accounts and practices in the paper, accountants could learn more about various practices in accounting.

It seemed that the greatest obstacle would be finding a way to describe the concepts, rather than just providing examples of when the principle would (and would not) be applicable. This was the challenge that many committees, professors, and researchers would face over the next few years as they tried to compile a successful list of principles.

It was not until 1973 that the FASB was established, headed by chairman Marshall S. Armstrong. They were named the authority on accounting later that year by the SEC. In 1973, the first purpose was established for financial statements, with the Study Group agreeing that statements should 'provide information useful for making economic decisions'. They further stated that the financial statements should be written in a way they could be understood by and offer insight to people that had limited ability, authority, or resources to understand the company's day-to-day movements. There were also a group of seven characteristics that dictated what financial statements should include to better satisfy the needs of readers.

From here, the board was presented with the challenge of classifying assets and liabilities appropriately. They published bulletins that discussed how reserves should be accounted for, whether advertising strategies should be counted as an asset or liability, and more. From here, the matching principle was established to prevent companies from unethically 'padding' some periods by adding more revenue than expenses. The committee carried on like this for years, slowly researching ideas to carefully build a framework. Today, the Federal Accounting

Standards Board remains a major authority on the generally accepted accounting principle. They also keep current with the latest challenges and accounting standards, which may change periodically from time to time to better reflect changes like the economy, valuation techniques, or new information that may change the standard for the way financial information is reported.

All the principles contained in the following chapters are modeled after the most current and up-to-date information available.

Important Terms

Before jumping into the basic principles of accounting, here are some general terms that you'll want to understand.

Assets

Assets are any resources controlled by a person or business entity that has economic value. This includes cash and accounts receivable, as well as things like securities, inventory, real estate, office equipment, land, and any other property that holds value.

Even though assets have a monetary value, they are grouped separately for a clearer snapshot of a company's value.

- Current assets describe a company's cash and assets of liquid value. Liquid assets are those that can be quickly converted to cash in the event of a financial emergency or liquidation. For example, a company's stocks, marketable securities, tax refunds, certificates of deposit, promissory notes, accounts receivables, and accrued income.

- Long-term assets are those that a company will use over a period of time. These often depreciate with time and might include things like equipment, real estate, vehicles, or manufacturing buildings. Long-term assets are also called fixed assets.

- Prepaid and deferred assets describe expenditures for future costs. Prepaid and deferred assets are not necessarily a benefit—they are usually rent, insurance, or other bills that a company pays ahead of time. They can also be described as advance payments. These payments are only assets until they become current—then the prepayments are moved over to the expenses area.

- Intangible assets are those that cannot be assigned a monetary value. This includes items like copyrights, patents, trademarks, and goodwill.

Liabilities

Liabilities describe any cash outflow that a business or entity already owes. Liabilities represent outflows of cash, especially those related to settling an outside debt. Even though a company has not always paid the liability right away, it is reported because they are responsible for that debt. Liabilities include debts to works such as wages paid out, as well as accounts payable, taxes, deferred revenues, and accrued expenses. Liabilities are classified as either current or long-term, with current liabilities being due within the next year and long-term liabilities being due over a longer period.

Equity

A business' equity is any remaining interest in its assets after all liabilities have been taken away. This is the amount that the business owes to owners and shareholders, usually represented as common stock and preferred stock. You can calculate the equity of a business by subtracting a company's liabilities from its assets. Equity may also be called shareholders' equity, net worth, or book value.

Revenues

Revenues are the inflow of wealth or economic benefit of a company. This includes a decrease in liabilities (which increases equity), improvement of an existing asset, or an inflow of wealth from the sale of goods or services. Even though contributions from shareholders, partners, and owners is an inflow of cash, it is not considered revenue as it did not come from the company's operations.

Expenses

The outflow of wealth or decrease in economic benefit is considered expenses. This might include natural deterioration or depletion of an asset, expenses incurred from repairs or maintenance, or accruing liabilities that will eventually create an outflow of cash. Money that is distributed to shareholders, partners, and owners is not considered an expense. Expenses are those costs associated with revenue-generating activities only. Expenses are classified into different categories, including:

- Accrued expenses- Expenses that a company has not paid for yet.

- Fixed expenses- Payments that happen regularly, like rent.

- Variable expenses- Payments that change from period-to-period, like labor expenses.

- Operation expenses- Expenses that are necessary for operation, but unrelated to the production of products and services, such as property taxes, insurance, or marketing costs.

Accounts Payable

Accounts payable describes goods and services bought on credit from vendors. It is part of a company's current liabilities, as the owed amount is expected to be paid for in less than a year. Once accounts payable is settled, it represents an outflow for the company.

Accounts Receivable

Accounts receivable is a current asset owed to the company by a customer for goods or services on credit. Usually, the amount is not listed on the balance sheet until the customer has been billed for the services. Companies notify customers of accounts owed using an invoice.

Capital

Capital is an asset's financial value, whether it is cash or goods. A company's working capital dictates what they can use to invest or distribute to shareholders. It is the current assets less the current liabilities or the money left over after debts in the current period are settled. Capital changes can also include contributions of the owners as investments, including their initial and additional contributions, as well as any withdrawals that they make for themselves or as dividends. Increases in the capital are realized through contributions and income, while decreases are realized through owner withdrawals and expenses.

General Ledger

The general ledger is a full record of any financial transaction over a company's entire lifetime. Usually, statements of cash flows and balance statements are made by reviewing and compiling data from the general ledger over a period of time.

Retained Earnings

Retained earnings usually describe those earnings that a company is able to re-invest in their company or set aside to accrue interest. Some companies may also create a retained earnings account. The retained earnings account signifies to readers of the financial plan that the company has an intended purpose for those earnings. For example, if a company is setting aside money to expand or purchase a new building, it would sit in the retained earnings account until the amount is sufficient enough to pay for the expansion.

Credits, Debits, and Double-Entry Accounting

Double-entry accounting is generally used by businesses because entries always affect at least two different accounts. For example, when a company buys supplies, it affects the cash account and the supplies account or the accounts payable account and the supplies account, depending on if they are paying for the supplies now or in the future.

The double-entry system works using debits and credits. Debits are listed on the left side of the account and credits are listed on the right. Debits increase assets or decrease liabilities, while credits decrease assets or increase liabilities.

It can be tricky to remember which accounts are credited and which are debited. However, there are a few acronyms you can use to remember this information.

Debits increase DEAL accounts, or Dividends, Expenses, Assets, and Losses. These accounts are also decreased by credits.

Credits increase GIRLS accounts or Gains, Income, Revenues, Liabilities, and Stockholders' (Owner's) Equity. These accounts are also decreased by debits.

Accounting Principles: Just for General Accounting?

Even though this book will focus heavily on the way that business' apply the generally accepted accounting principles to their accounting processes, many of these principles can also be applied to other types of accounting as well. It's important to remember that accounting principles is a broad, sweeping definition of some basic principles rather than a specific set of rules that must be followed. They can be applied to managerial accounting, tax accounting, and even personal accounting. However, it is important that those rules that are applied overlap with standards.

There are less rigorous standards for personal accounting and managerial accounting than tax accounting. In the case of tax accounting, businesses are held liable for their recognized revenue during the year and provides that information to the Internal Revenue Service. If the company has paid a significant amount in their taxes due over the year, they may end up owing more or less than anticipated. Being familiar with the principles used in general accounting helps with tax accounting because companies still must allocate their revenue and expenses appropriately to reflect what is going on in their business.

The principles can be applied to personal accounting as well, though many people use a cash accounting method that does not necessarily reflect all the principles. However, it is still important to match income to expenses, particularly as you decide how much to pay on which bills each month, the amount to be saved, how much to invest, and what you'd like to set aside for your own enjoyment.

For managerial accounting, following the principles is less important from a legal standpoint and more important for helping a business see its true standings. It is ethical and legal for a company to choose the methods they use on their own reports, but only if these reports are never shared with potential investors, creditors, or other external sources that are not aware of the company's financial practices. However, if a company does choose to use different account method for internal operations, it is important that owners, managers, and other decision-makers within the company are aware of both sets of financial statements. Otherwise, it can be difficult to see the full picture and determine how decisions now are going to affect the way that cash flows in and out of the company in the future.

One of the reasons accounting can be intimidating is because people do not always have a basic knowledge of what accounting is or how it works. By looking over these terms, you should have a clearer picture of how different elements of accounting tie in together. Next, we'll take a look at accounting methods before diving into the principles of accounting.

CHAPTER 2

An Introduction to Accounting Methods and Statements

An accounting method is a process that a business uses when reporting their income and expenses. In the United States, the two methods of accounting accepted by the Internal Revenue Service (IRS) are cash accounting and accrual accounting. Most people use the cash method of accounting when recording expenses. It is also the method most commonly used by small businesses. According to the regulations of the IRS, businesses that have over $5 million in sales annually are required to use the accrual accounting method. When a business is especially large, the accrual method offers a more accurate portrayal of their finances. These methods are used whenever a company completes its accounting statements. Each accounting statement offers insight into a business' financial stability, cash flow, sales and expenses, and other information over a given time period.

Cash Accounting Method

The cash basis of accounting is the simpler of the two methods. Revenues and expenditures are recorded when received and sent, rather than anticipating when they will be received and sent. This is straightforward and less confusing, especially for smaller businesses that may not have as much revenue and who do not retain large amounts of inventory. When people are writing a balance sheet or considering personal finances, they often compare their current amounts of cash in hand to the debts that they currently owe, rather than looking to the future.

Even though the cash accounting method is easier for small businesses to use, it is not the preferred method of the IRS for larger companies. This is because it is easy to alter payments when using the cash basis method of accounting. For example, a company might alter its revenue by receiving a check from a customer and holding onto it until the next fiscal year to avoid paying taxes on the amount. A company might also pay suppliers early so they can recognize more expense in the current year, which would also reduce the amount of taxable income. These are unethical behaviors that are strictly prohibited by the IRS, however, it is difficult to detect this type of behavior.

This does not mean that all delaying of reporting is unethical. For example, it is not uncommon for businesses to have a spike in sales during the holiday season. Some companies may not recognize the sales until the following fiscal year, especially if the cash receipts for credit card payments and checks will not be processed in time to be added to the current year's financial reports.

As it is easy to misconstrue financial information using the cash accounting method, there are limits on the people and businesses allowed to use it. Tax shelters and C corporations are prohibited from using the cash method. However, entities that have less than $25,000,000 in gross receipts for the last three tax years can use this method. Businesses that provide a personal service and receive at least 95% of their revenues related to their provided services may also use the cash method.

How to Use the Cash Accounting Method

The two most common statements for businesses using the cash accounting method are the income statement and the balance sheet. The income statement is produced monthly and it details all activity within that accounting period. For example, a graphic designer might complete work for a company on their website at the end of June. They would record any resources used and their time in the current month of June when they complete the work. However, if the client does not pay until August, then they would not record the payment for services until August.

The balance sheet of a company using the cash method will not show accounts payable or accounts receivable, as they do not calculate future revenues and expenditures. It also does not report information on inventory or work that is done in the current period, unless the customer pays for the work in the same period.

When creating a cash basis income statement, it is important that it is distinguishable from an accrual basis statement, particularly because the changes are vastly different and the way a statement is prepared effects the way it can be interpreted. Most companies using this method change their heading for statements. For example, the might write their company name, go down a line and write "Cash Basis Income Statement" and then go down another line and write 'for the month ended (date)'. Additionally, rather than labeling the results of the income statement as 'net income', it should be labeled as 'cash basis net income'. The reason for this is that the net income of companies using cash basis accounting can change drastically from one month to the next. Finally, in the disclosure section, it should be disclosed that the statement is a cash basis, meaning it has not been prepared using generally accepted accounting principles.

For the majority of this book, we will focus on the accrual basis system of accounting. As cash basis accounting is not as closely regulated as accrual basis accounting, it is easier for results to be misconstrued and misinterpreted. Sometimes, companies that use cash basis accounting for their books may create internal reports using accrual basis accounting. This can be done making a series of adjustments after reviewing the books. This helps make more informed decisions about the business, as it can be difficult to interpret a cash-basis statement, especially by companies that enter service contracts or get prepaid for services.

To make information relevant to accrual basis account, the revenue and expenses must be adjusted. For the revenue account, the following adjustments should be made:

- Receivables from customers that have paid bills should be subtracted

- Cash deposits for which the service or good has not been provided should be subtracted

- Bills that have been invoiced for work done in the period should be added

- Products/services that have been earned but not paid for should be added

To adjust the expenses for accrual basis accounting, the following changes should be made:

- Payments for expenses of a previous period should be subtracted

- Deposits for expenses that have not yet been paid should be subtracted

- Accumulated expenses that have not yet been invoiced by suppliers should be added

- Supplier invoices for the present period should be added

- Amortization, depreciation expense, and other non-cash expenses should be added

When a cash basis company undergoes an audit, they often must prepare their statements in this way. Auditors will not certify income statements that have been prepared according to cash accounting.

Accrual Accounting Method

The accrual method of accounting reports income and expenses when they are earned and incurred, rather than waiting until debts are paid. The biggest problem with the accrual method of accounting is that companies must make estimates. One of the biggest differences is the recognition that not all customers will pay the debt on time, in full, or at all. For this reason, companies that use the accrual method of accounting also have an account recorded as a bad debt expense.

Once a business generates a lot of sales, accrual accounting gives stockholders, investors, and creditors a better idea of how well the company is performing financially. It works well for companies that have lengthy contracts as well since there might not be as clear of a picture with the cash method of accounting.

Let's use a construction company as an example. Usually, construction companies receive at least a partial payment up front to help cover labor costs and the costs of materials. Rather than waiting to list additional revenue, they would list the percentage of the project complete at the time of the statement and its value, including income from the estimated payment of that percentage of the project and expenses from estimated materials and cost of labor for that portion of the project. This is spanned across the entire project, so there is an accurate reflection of cash inflows and outflows through the project.

If a cash method of accounting is used, the construction company might recognize a project when they schedule it. However, by recognizing revenue in the first month, their incoming revenue is going to show significantly less for the months they are working on that project. This would make it hard to attract investors or find loans if necessary during this time because the company looks like it does not have any revenue coming in. You'll learn more about how to do the accrual method of accounting in the next chapter as we go over some of the principles of accounting and how they should be applied.

Commonly Used Accounting Statements

The purpose of an accounting statement is to communicate certain information about a business. There are several types of statement, each of them containing specific information.

The Balance Sheet

The balance sheet, or statement of financial position, shows a business' assets, liabilities, and equity at a certain time. It is a current snapshot of earnings. Usually, people who use the information on the balance sheet might use it to calculate a company's risk regarding financing, credit, business, and liquidity. The goal of a balance sheet is to create balance. Current assets and non-current assets should equal the total amount of liabilities and equity.

The Income Statement

Also called the Profit and Loss Statement, this communicates information about a set amount of time. For example, a company might calculate an income statement for how they have performed monthly to track changes in their business. This is a statement of income and expense, including any amount the business has earned over that time from dividend income or selling goods and services or expenses including rental charges, salaries, and wages paid out, or depreciation. It is all the income and expenses that a business has from the cost of operating. This statement is used to calculate net profit (or loss) by subtracting the total expenses from the total income.

Cash Flow Statement

The statement of cash flows tracks how actual cash flows and bank balances change within a certain amount of time. It answers the questions of where the money is coming from or will be coming from, as well as where it was spent or will be spent. Three elements are needed for this statement, including operating activities, investing activities, and financing activities. Operating activities include flow from primary activities like the sale of goods or services. Investing activities include cash flow from the sale or purchase of assets other than inventory, including buying new office equipment of the sale of land. Financing activities include cash inflow or outflow from repaying or raising capital, as well as payments of dividends and interest to shareholders and owners. Over time, these show the net (overall) change in cash flow for the selected period.

Statement of Retained Earnings

Also referred to as the statement of changes in equity, which reports the amount the owners' equity in a certain period of time. This reports information like gains and losses in equity, such as those calculated by the revaluation of surpluses, net profit or loss found in the income statement, repaid or issued share capital during the period, and payments of dividends. The statement of retained earnings might also detail the effects of accounting error corrections or changes in accounting policies.

Notes to Financial Statements

In addition to the different financial statements, this area is included as a supplement to the financial documents. These notes contain disclosures that are required according to accounting standards. These standards report on any changes in accounting methods, breakdown line items, and support computations. Companies may also include information about significant profit or loss or changes that may result in profit or loss in the future. The notes to financial statements align with the idea of full transparency and allow for more accurate and honest financial reporting.

Relationships Between Financial Statements

When preparing financial statements, accountants use a specific order because information on some of the sheets carries over to the others.

The total revenue less the cost of goods sold represents gross profit. From the gross profit, companies subtract the sum of their total expenses. This helps them arrive at company earnings before tax. After taxes are removed, the amount left over is called the net earnings. Here's an example of what the basic income statement might look like:

Income Statement	
Revenue	105,000
Cost of Goods Sold	21,625
Gross Profit	83,375
Expenses	
Salaries and Benefits	25,600
Rent and Overhead	10,215
Depreciation and Amortization	5,600
Interest	2,700
Total Expenses	44,115
Earnings Before Tax	39,260
Taxes	3,215
Net Earnings	36,045

When the income statement is balanced, the net earnings represent the amount of money that a company has leftover from their operations. The net earnings represent a change in equity, or the amount of money that a company has after they have settled liabilities, paid out wages, and handled other responsibilities. When you create the balance sheet, the amount from net earnings is recorded as retained earnings that are calculated into stockholder's equity.

Before you begin the balance sheet, you'll need to create a statement of owner's equity. The owner's equity is a simpler sheet, as there are fewer columns to consider. Total capital is added to net earnings and additional contributions, such as an owner putting more capital into the company. After entering that money, owners also can withdraw it as they see fit. The number of withdrawals is subtracted from the total amount of equity and the final number is capital. This needs to be prepared before the balance sheet, as both the capital and the stockholders' equity will be on the balance sheet. The net income is also used when creating the cash flow statement.

Once the balance sheet is finalized, you can begin working on the statement of cash flows. If everything has been done correctly, the amounts on the statement of cash flows should be the sum of cash from operations, investing, and financing, as represented on the other financial sheets. When the amounts on these sheets all align, you know the books are properly balanced.

When everything is properly balanced, the results support the calculations you have done.

Finally, the notes to financial statements should support any calculations you have done or provide additional information relevant to understanding and interpreting the financial statement. You'll find out more about what should be included in these notes to financial statements in the chapter on the principle of full disclosure.

Now that you have a clear picture of the fundamentals, it's time to move on to the principles of accounting. Each of these principles should be applied to the accounting process whether you are analyzing or creating financial statements. By using them, you'll have a clearer picture of the methods used and how the numbers on accounting statements can be interpreted. After you've finished reading, be sure to check out the final chapters on applying what you've learned to the accounting cycle and accounting ratios.

Before you can practice accounting effectively, it's important to know the basic principles that are accepted as authority. These principles govern the field of accounting. When businesses do not adhere to these principles, it makes it more likely that they will be accused of unethical practices and that their reporting methods will be called into question, whether in the form of public scrutiny or an external audit.

CHAPTER 3

The Accrual Principle

Businesses that conduct a large number of transactions generally use the accrual method of accounting. The accrual principle applies to the accrual method of accounting, when businesses account for incoming and outgoing cash in the same period they become aware of them, rather than waiting until they make the payment or receive cash.

What is the Accrual Principle?

The accrual principle states that businesses should report transactions in the same period when they occur, instead of waiting until the time period when the cash flow is recognized. This principle forms the foundation for the accrual basis of accounting.

This is important because, without the accrual method, the information would be reported in the time period when the cash flows were incurred. This is inaccurate and can be misleading. Here's a look at how this would be applied when creating a financial document:

Company LMN offers customers a discount for paying their debts early. Company DEF owes company LMN $1000 for services on their website. The invoice was sent on July 28 but was not paid until August 8. This is what the entries may look like.

July 28	Accounts Receivable	1000	
	Service Revenue		1000
	Revenue earned for services		
Jul 8	Cash	1000	
	Accounts Receivable		1000
	Payment on revenue		

Note that these entries are going to appear on separate monthly balance sheets. However, as the work was completed in July, it should be recorded as revenue for that month. The accounts receivable amount is considered a debit at first, as it adds to the positive value of the company and is still considered an asset, even though that amount is not paid. When the account is paid, the accounts receivable account is credited and the cash account is debited because it is now cash on hand. The assets for the company will not change but there is a clearer picture of the true income and expenses of the given period. You can apply the accrual principle in the following ways:

- Recording expenses when incurred instead of upon sending payment

- Recording revenue after invoicing instead of when payment is received

- Recording wages as they are earned, rather than when the employee is paid

- Recording commission when earned instead of when paid

- Recording estimates of bad debt upon invoice, rather than when non-payment becomes apparent

- Recording depreciation over the useful life of an asset instead of charging the entire amount to the period it was purchased in

When the accrual method is used properly, revenue and expense information can be reported without delays and distortions caused by waiting for cash flows or postponing payment for something.

Why the Accrual Principle is Useful

For Complex Transactions

The average small business has small transactions. For example, a store that sells homemade candles would keep relatively simple ledgers. As they did not generate a lot of revenue, it would be easier to track revenue from sales and expenses related to sales. When a company grows, however, they must start to think about things like expanding their business and keeping up with the higher demands of business. They may need to hire additional employees, buy more space, or purchase more equipment. Even though these are positive events because they will make a business more profitable, they also add to the complexity of a company's financial transactions.

When complex methods are used, it becomes more difficult to understand the financial events of a company that uses a cash accounting method. Accrual accounting gives a better picture of complex business practices. This is important for calculating ratios and metrics like the net income, operating margin, and gross profit margin.

Financial Reports Remain Consistent and Accurate

The cash accounting principle focuses more on the assets on hand, rather than the assets that have been accrued in a month. For example, when a client fails to pay an account, the amount of time, work, and material that went into providing their good or service are not realized in cash accounting. However, this makes it harder to account for the potential revenue of a business each month. If this amount is never recorded, then that work is not accounted for either.

When businesses apply the accrual principle, they realize the expected payment and the resources used to provide the good or service in the same month. This makes it easier to track a company's performance from month to month. If they did not have as much revenue one month, they can track it to those occurrences rather than having to review months of accounting statements to find the entry that reflects the changes.

When Trading Stock

While companies are allowed to seek out individual investors, companies cannot sell stocks as a publicly traded company unless they use the accrual method of accounting. As the accrual method gives a clearer, more honest picture of a company's financial standings, it allows stockholders a better ability to analyze the inner workings of a company.

The Accrual Principle and Matching Principle

The accrual principle is also used by businesses that have a high volume of sales because it helps them use the matching principle easier. The matching principle states that the cost of providing a service or producing a good should be realized in the same period as related revenue.

For example, a company would apply both principles when an employee completes work for them. They would make an entry for the wages account and cash account to pay the employee for work completed on the site. They would also record the revenue for the work done. If there was an additional profit after the employee was paid, they add it to the income account.

The Accrual Principle and the Revenue Recognition Principle

The accrual principle aligns with the revenue recognition principle as well. Instead of waiting for payment to be received after a service is completed, accountants realize them in the period when they happened. The revenue recognition principle also aligns with the matching principle, as this means the expenses related to providing a good or service must also be recorded in the same period when revenue is recognized.

Limitations of the Accrual Principle

The greatest limitation is that when using accrual accounting, companies appear to have cash flow even when they do not. If there is a significant number of accounts that do not pay, a company may even go bankrupt because they believe they are performing better financially than they truly are.

In the case of a small start-up, this could be disastrous. If a company shows cash inflows that have not happened, they may falsely believe there are enough resources on hand to fulfill another order. Extreme cash shortages can even lead to bankruptcy, especially as the company is unable to fulfill orders and customers begin to file complaints. They may also lose credibility, which makes it harder to attract new business.

CHAPTER 4

The Conservatism Principle

Being conservative simply means taking precautions. In business, it is important to protect your assets. There are risks associated with any type of business. Customers may cancel their regular accounts and there will be some people that do not pay debts. Even companies that only allow payments upfront can find themselves struggling with problems like damaged or unsellable inventory, canceled credit card and check payments, and other issues. The conservatism provides a little protection, especially for companies that have high risks associated with doing business.

What is the Conservatism Principle?

Conservatism is the idea that liabilities and expenses should be recorded as soon as possible. It may also be referred to as the prudence concept or the conservatism concept. For example, if a company receives their electric bill in the middle of the month, but they do not have to pay it until the following month, they should still record it in the month received. These are amounts that a company owes, regardless of what happens and it is unlikely they are not going to pay them.

On the other side of the conservatism principle, assets and revenues should only be recorded once a company is sure they will occur. For example, they might not record a new customer's account as revenue until they are sure the account is being paid.

Deciding How Often to Use the Conservatism Principle

Of course, conservatism must be used with the conservatism principle. If a company regularly reports losses and postpones gains, it can make the state of their company appear worse than it is, which can lead to a lower net worth or valuation. Companies could also postpone more of their debts while recording more revenues, which would also create an unfair valuation, this one being higher than expected.

The best way for companies to use conservatism is to analyze their previous transactions and take note of trends. Estimates are generally used to create accounts that create a paper trail for the conservatism principle. This is important should the company ever be audited, especially if they are using the conservatism principle unethically. For example, a company could create an allowance for doubtful accounts that offsets the accounts receivable to avoid recognizing too much revenue. If they generally have 2% of customers that do not pay their accounts on time or in full, they would determine the amount of 2% of their revenue. The amount would be debited to the allowance for doubtful accounts and credited to accounts receivable.

The Conservatism Principle and the Lower Cost or Market Rule

The conservatism principle also uses the lower of cost or market rule. Basically, this means that inventory should always be recorded as the amount to acquire it rather than the amount it is sold at. The alternative to this is listing at market value. Rather than listing inventory at its potential, listing it at its actual value respects the conservatism principle. This aligns with the idea that companies should lower their risk when completing their financials by protecting their assets.

Let's take a look at these principles in action. Imagine that a company sells exclusive tapestries. They have unique designs and only run a limited number of each item. One tapestry is intended to be sold for $450 and it cost the company $40 to make each tapestry. The company decides to run only 100 of these tapestries.

If the potential amount the tapestries could make was considered, that would be $45,000. If the company credited the inventory account $45,000 and the blanket was one of their worst sellers, they may have to come down in price. That could cause a significant reduction in the valuation of the inventory. Since inventory is considered an asset, this means the company is worth less than it was valuated at. By contrast, if the company experiences greater sales revenue than anticipated with the tapestry, they can realize this accurately as profit. It also prevents the risk of appearing to be losing revenue if their design does not sell.

The conservatism principle is an idea that does not need to be applied at all times. This is an area where there is some gray area. One good rule to follow is to consider how the financial will be affected by the sale of a service or good. If it is going to cause a valuation that is significantly greater or lower than the true value of the company, then the conservatism rule likely should not be applied. The goal is to create statements that reflect the company's financials as accurately as possible. Skewing information is unethical and in many cases, illegal.

CHAPTER 5

The Consistency Principle

It would be impossible to track the finances of a company who used the cash accounting method one month and the accrual method the next. The consistency principle states that companies should be consistent about the way they report their financial information. This creates transparency in their methods of reporting.

The exception to this rule is as a company learns that one method or the other may work better for their company. For example, successful small businesses often attract new clients over time. As their business grows, they may find the accrual method of accounting works best. To remain consistent, once they implement the accrual method of accounting, they should stick with it until another method proves itself more useful.

Of course, should a business choose to switch their accounting method, this should be noted in the full disclosure area of the financial statements. Failure to disclose creates an illusion, particularly the first months after the change with the differences in financial statements are likely to be significant. It is apparent a company is ignoring the consistency principle when more profits or revenues are accounted for than would normally be recognized. Usually, the operational activity levels remain the same and company profits increase exponentially.

Other Applications of the Consistency Principle

The consistency principle should also be applied to other decisions made when creating a financial statement, such as decisions about how to process transactions. For example, if a company were to create a doubtful allowance account for customers that did not pay their accounts for 2% of their revenue, they would need to recognize this 2% allowance for every financial period. They could not calculate 2% of revenue for one month and 5% the next. The exception would be situations where a company has proven that the trend changes their consistent actions. For example, companies might have a greater allowance for doubtful accounts during the holiday season, particularly those companies offering credit to customers that may not pay their accounts. If a company does find themselves losing more in doubtful accounts during the holidays, they would note that they have changed this for the current financial period to provide a more accurate overview of their projections.

The way that a company depreciates assets is something else that should stay consistent from accounting period to accounting period. There are three different depreciation methods; the straight-line method, the double-declining balance method, and the sum of years depreciation method. Once a company decides how an asset will best be depreciated, that same schedule should be followed for the asset's entire lifetime.

Benefits of Consistent Reporting

When companies report consistently, it gives a more accurate, honest portrayal of the financial movements of their company. Another major benefit is the ability to compare financial information. This comparison helps show upward or downward trends in a company's progress and helps make decisions. Additionally, using consistent methods makes it less likely that a company will go through an audit. Businesses that are audited will have a better paper trail and be less likely to have problems resulting from their audit. Finally, choosing a single method of reporting and sticking to it is more cost-efficient. Each time that an accounting strategy is switched, the affected employees must take the time to re-learn the new method and implement the new strategies. By sticking with consistent means of reporting, there is no additional cost of training or implementing new reporting methods.

The Consistency Principle and Ratios

The consistency principle is also important for the calculation of accurate ratios. Ratios are commonly used equations in accounting that are used to determine things like a company's liquidity or their average return on assets. This information is useful for many reasons. Some are important to creditors or banks that are considering loaning a business money in determining their creditworthiness and if the company has sufficient resources to make payments on the loan without going bankrupt. Stockholders might also look at a company's financial statements to understand potential returns on their investment and decide how much stock they want to buy from a company.

Finally, the consistency principle benefits people inside of an organization. It is not uncommon for internal financial reports to happen monthly, and even weekly in some businesses. These internal reports are used to help members of management make decisions about the company. They also contain information that can be used to create budget reports, identify problems, and create projections. If the information on the financial statements were not reported in the same way each month, it would create problems and make it harder to identify potential issues and run the business in general.

Properly Reporting Changes

The consistency principle exists as a guideline for companies to continue conducting business. If they fail to properly report when they change strategies, it causes confusion and discrepancies. To properly report a change, a company must create a note of the change. They must also disclose the reasons behind the change and any supporting reasons that give their change credibility, as well as the date of the change and how long the change will take place. For example, a company that has a higher rate of allowable accounts during the holiday season may note the trends affecting their change and the dates it would take place, more than likely November, December, and January.

CHAPTER 6

The Cost Principle

The cost principle is the idea that equity investments, assets, and liabilities should be recorded at original costs. While this is still considered an accounting principle, its use is limited and even considered controversial, as the cost of a company's assets does not necessarily reflect their financial standing at the present time. Most companies calculate the depreciation value of their assets and liabilities, which adjusts them to their fair value. However, there are other assets in a company that cannot be accounted for. For example, a trademark that is heavily associated with a company (without being paid for) cannot be assigned a value because it was not acquired in a transaction.

Depreciation of Assets

Companies that do use the cost principle might use it for new purchases but assign a useful life to that purchase. For example, they may estimate useful life of ten years on a new computer purchased in July for the office that costs $3,600. The computer would depreciate over the ten years at a rate of $360/year. From here, that amount would be spread across 12 months, for an equivalent of $30 per month. This means the value of the computer as an asset would be $3,600 in the month of July, then $3,570 for the month of August. When the asset is depreciated, the offset value is placed in the depreciation account.

Even using depreciation value can be flawed since the used value of an asset will not reflect its historical cost on its purchase date. Imagine that same computer was being sold after being used for 2 years. It is unlikely that the company will find someone to pay almost $3,000 for a computer that has been heavily used for two years, which is what the depreciation value would reflect.

There are several strategies that companies may use to calculate the depreciation of assets, including straight-line depreciation, double-declining balance depreciation, and sum of years depreciation. Depreciation is necessary to accurately reflect the potential liquidity of an item, should the company go bankrupt or face financial troubles and need to sell off their assets.

Straight Line Depreciation

The first step in calculating depreciation using this method is subtracting the salvage value of the item, which is the value of the item after it has been depreciated if it were to sell, from the total purchase price. This is the depreciable cost, which is the amount that the item is going to depreciate through its useful lifetime. For example, a piece of equipment that was purchased at $2,500 with a scrap value of $300 would depreciate by $2,200 over its useful lifetime.

Next, divide the depreciable cost by the number of years that the asset is expected to be used. For example, imagine that the $2,500 item was a piece of factory equipment that would be used for 10 years. The depreciable cost, therefore, would be $250 per year for ten years. Most companies account for their depreciable amounts once per year, when they are preparing financial statements, rather than spacing them out monthly. It is more efficient this way.

Double-Declining-Balance Method

To use this method, you'll need to know the useful life of the asset and its total costs. Start by dividing 100% by the number of years that the item has a useful life. Returning to the example above, an item with a useful life of ten years would be 10%. Then, multiply this number by 2 (20%). This is the annual depreciation of the item.

Next, take the purchase price of the item and multiply it by the annual depreciation. For an asset costing $2500, this would be $500. This will be done every year, so the amount depreciated will be different every year. In the first year, the balance would decline by $500, leaving a depreciable cost of $2,000. In the second year, the $2,000 would be multiplied by 20% and $400 would be subtracted. In the third year, $1,600 would be multiplied by 20% and $320 would be subtracted. This would continue until the balance of the depreciation value takes the cost below the salvage value.

This method is ideal for companies that are worried about long-term finances, as it depreciates the asset sooner and it does not continue depreciating through its entire lifetime. This method works better for certain purchases, depending on a company's financial standings and how much the depreciable value is going to affect the overall balance of their assets and liabilities.

Sum of Years Depreciation

The sum of years depreciation technique can be a little complicated, so it is best to create a spreadsheet or table to create a depreciation schedule. Begin by creating a table that has six columns. It should also have one row for each year of an asset's useful life.

The topmost row is going to contain the labels for each column as follows; beginning book value, total depreciable cost, depreciation rate, depreciation expenses, accumulated depreciation, ending book value. We'll use the same example as we have been using for this method, as well. In the first row, list the purchase price of the asset ($2,500).

Then, subtract the salvage value ($300) from the purchase price. Take the resulting number ($2,300) and enter it in all the rows under the Total Depreciable Cost heading. This would be 10 rows in this case, as there are 10 years in the useful life of the item.

To calculate the depreciation rate, calculate the sum of all the years in an asset's useful life. For this example, we'd add (1 + 2 + 3 + 4 + 5 + 6 + 7 + 8 + 9 + 10) for a total of 54. In the first year, divide the total by the last number (10). Place this in the second column and move down, dividing by 9 in the next row and 8 in the following, and so on and so forth.

To calculate depreciation value for each year, you multiply the total depreciable cost by the depreciation rate. The first would be $2,300/(10/54) or around $425.93. This is recorded in the depreciation expenses column. Subtract the depreciation from the depreciable cost to arrive at the ending book value. In this case, it would be $1,874.07. This is the ending book value for the first year, but also the beginning book value for the second. For the following years, use the beginning book value and multiply by the appropriate percentage each year. You record the total depreciation in the fifth column until you arrive at the total amount.

Amortization

While depreciation tracks the useful life of tangible assets like machinery, land, vehicles, and buildings, amortization spread the cost of an intangible asset over the cost of its useful life. Some common things that may be amortized include organizational costs, proprietary processes like copyrights, trademarks and patents, franchise agreements, and the cost of issuing bonds to raise capital. While there are several methods that a company may use to depreciate an asset, amortization is rather straightforward and uses a straight-line basis. Something else to note different from the depreciation process is that the immaterial items amortization is used for do not have a salvage value. Therefore, it is simple to calculate amortization. Take the total cost of the amortized item and divide it by its useful life. The resulting number is the amount that should be allocated to the amortization expense each year.

Depletion

The depletion method is similar to depreciation and amortization, though it is used less frequently. Depleting is used for the cost of natural resources. For example, a company that has access to an oil well for operations can use the oil well until it runs dry. The cost of setting up the well and making it ready for pumping can be spread across the entire useful life of the oil well.

Limitations of the Cost Principle

The cost principle also cannot be applied to financial investments. Rather than recording investments as they are at the time of investment, the amount must be adjusted to reflect the fair value for each new accounting period. For example, if a company offers a 1% return on investment to preferred shareholders, they are liable for the amount of the investment in addition to that 1%, so the total value is recorded.

As the cost principle is difficult to apply to historical cost without construing a company's true worth, it is generally reserved for short-term assets and liabilities. This might include office supplies or purchased materials for manufacturing. The risk of misleading reporting is most challenging in capital-intensive industries, particularly those where companies have a significant amount of long-term assets. To avoid muddling the financial statements, companies may not list these at historical cost and instead choose to depreciate them over time.

In some businesses, it is not uncommon for current assets to be traded for work or additional assets. For example, construction companies often trade in their old work vehicles for a new model, rather than realizing a total loss. In the event of a trade, the company recognizes the cost of the new vehicle as the cash value of the trade-in vehicle and any additional cash amount that needed to be paid for it.

Something else to note is that companies usually record amount paid, rather than the actual value of an asset. Otherwise, it would distort the balance sheet and might have unequal effects on the offsetting accounts.

One argument against the cost principle is that it does not reflect the current market value. However, most assets used in business depreciate over time instead of appreciating, so it is unlikely the company would ever realize the full value of the purchased asset. For example, even if they paid thousands less for an item, that asset is still going to depreciate over time. Even though there are some scenarios where market value might be a more accurate representation, the historical cost principle is used because it is more objective and reliable than the market place. It also does not fluctuate with the current financial market.

CHAPTER 7

The Economic Entity Principle

The economic entity principle establishes a very important distinction between businesses and the people who own them. This means all transactions carried out by the company with suppliers, customers, and other businesses must be related specifically to the entity that claims them in their general ledger. When an owner fails to separate personal transactions and business transactions, it has a negative effect on the balances in the accounts and makes it harder for the company to maintain trust with potential creditors, investors, and stockholders.

Why is the Economic Entity Principle Important?

The economic entity principle is important for keeping the finances of the company separate from its owners. If one of the owners bought a truck to use for delivery of their products, then the truck would be recorded as an asset and it would be credited to the cash account (or the accounts payable account) of the company. If one of the owners used their own money to buy a vehicle for personal use, however, this would not be recorded with the finances of the company.

The economic entity principle also has implications for a company's tax processes. For example, some items that have been bought for a business can be deducted from taxes. If a person works as a freelance writer, they would be able to purchase a laptop and use it for their business. However, if they used the laptop for business and personal use, they would not be able to claim it on their taxes. Likewise, some people run businesses out of their homes while they are bringing in revenue and trying to get their company off the ground. Using their home as an office space can be deducted, but only if they have an office in their home that is specifically used for work.

Finally, if a company did not separate its own finances from the personal finances of its owner, the financial statements would be unusable. It would be impossible to calculate important ratios or track how well the business was doing if financial transactions that did not belong to the company were muddled with the correct financial information.

Analyzing Transactions

For companies to effectively maintain records apart from its owners and other entities, its important that each maintains its own financial records (general ledger) and its own bank account. Sole proprietorships are the easiest to overlap since the owners of these businesses often mix their own transactions in with business transactions.

Even though entities exist separately, consolidated financial statements may be prepared. These statements reflect information on a group of entities that are owned by a single person or entity. This allows the owner to look over them all and determine total net worth.

It is not uncommon for new businesses to make the mistake of mingling their personal and business transactions. Once a business grows, an accountant is usually brought in to sort through transactions and balance the books appropriately so they reflect business transactions only. This initial analysis of receipts and transactions for the business is a necessary part of the accounting cycle that an entity must go through before creating financial statements. From here, entries are made in a journal and then the journal amounts are totaled to create accounts for the period for the general ledger.

Example: Personal Sales Outside of Business

Even a personal sale cannot be used for the business, even if the owner were to make a personal sale and invest their money as capital back in their business. For example, imagine that a shop sells boats and boating equipment, as well as offers a repair service. After seeing a picture of one of the owner's in front of their boat at the shop, a customer inquires about the boat and the owner ends up making a transaction with that customer, selling their personal boat for $14,200. The owner decides that even though this is personal revenue, they are passionate about their business and would like to invest that amount of capital.

Even though the owner intends to invest that capital, the transaction for the sale is not business conducted for the company. If the owner were to invest the capital, that would be recorded as a transaction. However, their personal boat did not take company resources to produce and the sale did not affect the company's inventory in any way. Therefore, it would not be ethical to list the capital as sales revenue. If the boat was recorded, it would drastically inflate the company's sales, especially because the boat would be realized as profit without any effects anywhere else in the company.

How Start-Ups Can Follow the Economic Entity Principle

Many start-ups begin as small operations with people offering a service or selling products themselves. When owners are the only people involved in the business, it is not uncommon for them to retain what they need for living and invest the rest in continuing work for their business. However, once a freelancer decides to become a business on paper and establish themselves, it is important to separate their goods.

It is not uncommon for new owners to use their personal bank account to accept payments and receive loan help, as well as to make purchases on their personal credit card. Unfortunately, the owner's personal accounts will likely have a variety of personal transactions mixed in with those from the business. The ideal situation is for an owner to establish themselves as a business first. Then, they can purchase a DBA (doing business as), which allows them to act as an entity on behalf of their company. They can then open a bank account, get a credit card, and process transactions under their businesses name. It is better for small business to do this sooner rather than later, as the more transactions that are mixed together, the more pain-staking the process of separating the business and personal transactions will be.

The Economic Entity Principle vs. Limited Liability

People would be less likely to start small businesses is everything was tied into their personal finances, especially as their purchases would be under close scrutiny. While the economic entity principle is designed to stop personal and business accounts from mingling, limited liability is the idea that owners of a business should not be held liable for bankruptcy if their company fails.

For example, imagine that company LMN had success with an eco-friendly product line. While there was significant interest, the interest was not from their usual customer base so company

LMN decided to create a child company, company QRS. Company QRS was successful but eventually went bankrupt and had to be liquidated. Company LMN would not be held liable, nor would its owners for the bankrupt business if there was a balance due after it was liquidated.

CHAPTER 8

Full Disclosure Principle

Full disclosure is providing readers of a financial statement with any information that may be relevant to interpreting a business' financial statements. Companies should look at this as a chance to explain their position and disclose anything that stockholders', creditors, or anyone else looking over their statements would want to know. For example, a period might show hundreds of thousands in losses of assets after a warehouse fire where a lot of inventory is lost. The full disclosure area would give readers a chance to understand the reason behind the loss of assets.

What Does Full Disclosure Entail?

Of course, the idea of 'full disclosure' may leave an inexperienced accountant feeling as if they have to disclose everything possible about a company. Any small detail could be considered important. For this reason, full disclosure is generally limited to those events that will have an impact on a company's financial results or financial position. In addition to monetary amounts, companies may disclose items that do not yet have a monetary value. For example, a business involved in a lawsuit expecting to pay out damages might not know how severe the cost of damages is going to be, so they may include this without quantifying it. Some other bits of information that might be included are material losses caused by the value of something significantly depreciating, changes in a relationship that has a significant amount of value within a company, or the details of a non-monetary transaction that might affect future financial reports.

Information for full disclosure may be in several places, including within item line descriptions on the balance sheet or income statement. Sometimes, accompanying disclosures are also included. Something to note is that while full disclosure is important, it is not generally used on internal financial reports created for use within a company. Management is usually aware of scenarios and might only want to see the major elements of the financial statement.

The full disclosure area often contains information about some important details of the company that stockholders may be interested in as well. For example, they might make a note about income taxes, stock options, or information regarding earnings per share. This type of information can be used to have a better idea of how the company is performing and communicate information about known ratios. Something to note is that this information is sometimes skewed slightly to attract potential investors. For example, a company might include its own financial interpretation of the company's standing in order to make its financial position appear better. This is meant to attract potential investors, especially those that are not familiar with the ratios or how to analyze the company's financial statements on their own.

Why is Full Disclosure Important?

Have you ever tried to make a decision without all the necessary information? For example, imagine that your friend's wife asked him to consider taking anger management classes or file for a divorce. The friend may be tired of trying, especially if things have been stressful between the husband and wife. After the divorce, the friend is upset because he learns his now ex-wife is pregnant. If he had known that there was a new child coming into the picture, he may have been more inclined to go to the anger management classes and try to resolve problems in the marriage.

Stakeholders do not have access to the same information as members of management and CEO's, as they do not have constant access to transactions and the flow of cash in and out of the company. They are also not involved in the decision-making process and may be unaware of the accounting practices followed by the company. Full disclosure gives them what is considered 'needed insight' into the company. It allows them to know the key points about decisions that were made or events, both financial and non-financial, that may affect the company's statements in the foreseeable future.

Where Can Full Disclosure Articles Be Found?

In addition to areas like the notes section of financial statements and supplementary schedules that are provided with the statements, full disclosure can be found in several other places. Any type of communications from the company outside of their usual financial reporting schedule may contain this information, including press releases, quarterly earnings reports, and other communications. When publicly-traded corporations file their annual report to the Securities and Exchange Commission (SEC) of the United States, they may also fill out Form 10-K. This is a section titled *Management's Discussion and Analysis* and it is used to report anything that the SEC may need to know when reviewing their submissions.

CHAPTER 9

The Going Concern Principle

The going concern principle indicates that a company should remain open and continue conducting business as usual. Think of it this way—would you want to give a business a loan if their liabilities heavily outweighed their assets and they were at risk of closing, liquidating, or going bankrupt? This principle helps protect investor's assets and help the financial stability of a company be determined.

What is the Going Concern Principle?

This principle indicates that a business is expected to keep conducting business as usual for the foreseeable future. As they do not have to liquidate assets or worry about selling off assets at low prices, accountants of these companies can defer certain expenses until later. By deferring certain expenses, the available assets can be allocated in the best way possible and in a way that encourages further growth. For example, a company may be able to put more money into their inventory by postponing their payment until the next period, which can help them keep up with sales and generate more revenue.

The going concern principle cannot be applied if there is significant information that points toward the company being unable to meet its financial obligations. For example, if a company cannot pay for its liabilities when they are due without restructuring their debt or selling a substantial number of assets, the going concern principle would not be used. If companies continued to operate despite them not having a going concern, it would be unethical. They would be taking on more debt without the ability (and sometimes without the intent) to pay their liabilities. Companies may do this sometimes if they are in doubt about how bad their financials are, but that does not make it an ethical practice, especially if they do not disclose their poor financial status to stockholders.

What Happens When a Company Doesn't Have Going Concern?

When an accountant believes a company cannot use the going concern principle, they must decide if assets are impaired. This is done with an audit. The audit evaluates the financials of a company and decides if an asset cannot be used to continue producing revenue for the company. When assets are impaired, the amount of their liquidation value is recorded, which is the amount that the asset could be sold for in a quick sale to help pay off some of the company's liabilities and settle some debts before bankruptcy is declared or the company closes its doors. Usually, the liquidation value of an asset is much lower than the current value. It is based on how quickly the asset can be sold, rather than what it costs at current market value. Liquidation companies are not focused on getting the most of assets—they are just focused on getting rid of them.

When an entity continues to be a going concern, therefore, the valuation of their assets is significantly higher than the liquidation value of assets. They are allowed to report the higher values because the assets are either currently being used (in the case of buildings, machinery, or vehicles that might be used to store inventory or fulfill services) are being used to generate revenue and the company is not interested in the liquidation value of these items. In the case of inventory, the cost is reported for the potential sales to break even (without making a loss) as long as the company is believed to be capable of continuing to conduct business in the future.

When a company's going concern is brought into question, it is not uncommon for a third-party auditor to be brought in to analyze statements. A company is considered to have a going concern as long as they are expected to stay open for at least one year following the period of the financial statements being audited. Some things that may be brought into question include:

- Legal proceedings where the company is a defendant

- Loan defaults by the business

- A series of losses or other negative trends from operating

- Long-term commitments that are uneconomical to consider meeting

- Denial of trade credit from suppliers

Any of these events can be red flags, but none can be used to determine whether a company has going concern on its own. When a company intends to remain open but an auditor will not grant them going concern, a company may have a third party guarantee the business' debts or agree to give them additional financing as needed. This creates a reasonable assurance that the business will continue to function without accruing a significant amount of debt. Under the GAAS, companies that can find a third-party guarantor are granted an additional one-year period to continue business operations under the going concern principle.

However, companies that are not granted going concern may find it difficult to find a third-party guarantor, as the guarantor may be concerned about the business' actions and becoming liable for debts, should the entity not begin generating revenue as expected.

Allowances Under the Going Concern Principle

When an entity has going concern, they are free to operate as if they will be around to pay their debts. They can enter into agreements with suppliers, take advance payments for contracts, and purchase more inventory and assets. They are also allowed to do things like spread the depreciation value across the useful life of an asset and issue stock in exchange for capital to invest in their business.

Of course, it's important to remember that the going concern principle only pertains to the entity as a whole. If a company decides to reduce some of their assets to liquidation value and continue with other operations, they can still operate under going concern as long as their other operations are significant enough to produce revenue that will allow operation of the business. When there is a question of going concern, it is important for companies to disclose this information in their financial statements, as this can significantly impact the companies willing to continue doing business with them.

The Going Concern Principle in Action

There are several examples that can be used to help determine a company's going concern. For example, imagine that well-known company Microsoft is suing a private tech company for violating the copyright in its software package. If the software package was the only source of revenue for the company and auditors expect Microsoft to win, that company would likely not be given going concern. Losing the lawsuit would destroy their entire company and they would likely go out of business following the legal proceedings.

A real-life example happened in the early 2000s when well-known auto manufacturer General Motors was expected to declare bankruptcy around the world because of the severity of their financial condition. The federal government stepped in as a guarantor for the company's next year of operation, successfully bailing them out of trouble. GM would not have been able to attain going concern status, but with the bailout, they were expected to continue operating.

If part of a company's revenue is severely impacted, it does not necessarily mean they cannot achieve the status of going concern. For example, the United States government raided the Gibson Guitar factory in 2011 to confiscate endangered wood the company had smuggled into the country. Over $250,000 of inventory was confiscated and the company also had to pay large fines for their role in violating international laws. As the Gibson Guitar company is well-established, the steep fines and confiscated inventory did not affect their ability to maintain a status as a company with going concern.

CHAPTER 10

The Matching Principle

If a company did not use the matching principle for revenues and expenses, it would be nearly impossible to create a balance sheet that actually balanced. It would also make it difficult to use accounting ratios to evaluate a company since the positives and negatives wouldn't accurately track cash flow between different periods. For this reason, companies use the matching principle. The expenses incurred when making revenue are recorded in the same period as the revenue, regardless of when the actual money is received.

What is the Matching Principle?

The matching principle states that revenues and the expenses related to generating these revenues are matched in the same period, rather than being reported separately. The purpose of that matching principle is to create a cause-and-effect style of relationship that makes it easier to determine costs associated with generating revenue. The matching principle aligns with the principle of accrual basis accounting, as the revenue and expenses are reported in the same period.

When the periods are not matched, it makes it difficult to create a balance sheet or income statement, as the debits and credits will not balance out. This might be applied to commission or bonuses, which employees earn after the initial sale or performance review, as well as to depreciation, employee wages, and accrued expenses. The matching principle is not used for cash accounting, as cash accounting does not require debits and credits to be accounted for in the same period. It focuses more on what a company has at the current time.

Additional Uses of the Matching Principle

In addition to being used for revenues and expenses, the matching principle is applied to all inflows and their related outflows, including normal business operations. For example, imagine that a company pays a bonus annually depending on how well they performed during that fiscal year. Since the amount is not calculated until after the company financial statements have been completed for the year, payment doesn't occur until the next accounting period. Rather than accounting for the bonus in one year and accounting for the payout the next, which would cause an imbalance in assets and liabilities, the company accounts for both payments in the same period. The bonus is debited to a bonus payable account and the cash value is credited. When the bonus is paid out, the bonuses payable account is credited and the bonus expense is debited. Both of these actions keep the balance sheet in a state of balance.

Limitations of the Matching Principle

The one limitation of the matching principle is that it does not give a full picture of a company's financial standings when looking at the income statement. The cash flow statement should also be looked at since this is where companies can see the specific incoming and outgoing revenue. This is important for financial planning, especially if a company has a large payment due.

Systematic Allocation and the Matching Principle

Even though the matching principle is used to show cause-and-effect relationships in the various transactions of a business, it does not always show clear benefits. For example, companies may create a marketing expense so they can promote their business and attract new customers. However, the number of customers brought in cannot be quantified, especially since the additional revenue will be spaced out. To avoid allocating too much of the marketing expense in one period, the company accounts for the life of the campaign and spreads the total cost out over the length of the campaign. For example, a 2-year campaign that costs $5,000 would have $2,500 allocated in one period and $2,500 allocated in the next.

This same allocation technique could also apply to the purchase of a new factory so the company can expand its line and produce more goods. Even though the factory will have a significant impact on generating inventory and bringing in revenue, the total effect cannot be measured because the transactions will be spaced out. Therefore, the company might say the factory has a useful life of 15 years and spread the total cost out over that period.

CHAPTER 11

The Materiality Principle

Many investors and creditors would become easily frustrated if the financial statements were a mess, with plenty of small details included that really made no difference in the financial standings of the company. Including those items that have insignificant value is going to make it harder to understand the statements. The materiality principle is created for scenarios when adhering to one of the GAAP's (generally accepted accounting principles) would cause confusion in the statement. It is also created for scenarios when a company decides not to follow one of the principles. Materiality can also be interpreted as significance since businesses do not have to adhere to all the principles unless failing to do so would have a significant impact on their financial statement.

What is the Materiality Principle?

The materiality principle is the guideline that companies may ignore an accounting standard if the overall impact has a small impact on financial statements, in the way that by ignoring the guideline, people are not misled when reading the financial statements. The dispute comes from distinguishing items that are material in nature from those that are immaterial.

Even though there are no specific guidelines for adhering to the materiality principle, the Securities and Exchange Commission (SEC) of the United States recommends entities report individual assets that represent at least 5% of values. Items that will make a net profit a net loss, or vice versa, should also be recorded regardless of the size of the items. Additionally, when reporting transactions, they should be considered material if the transaction would have a significant impact on a ratio.

For example, a company may pay $100 for a post office box for six months. Rather than dividing this into six periods and reporting the small amount each period, the cost of the PO box would be accounted for in the period when the expense was paid. This is so insignificant to a large company that its presence (or lack of) is not going to impact the overall financial statement.

Of course, the idea of materiality depends on an entity's size. While a multi-national company that does billions in sales annually might consider a $500,000 transaction immaterial, this amount could easily exceed the revenues made by a local firm.

For the smaller company, that amount would be considered material, but the larger company could easily count this as immaterial money.

The materiality principle is most applicable when accountants are deciding which transactions should be recorded while closing out accounts for the month. By reducing the number of transactions that must be listed, taking away immaterial items helps reduce the amount of time needed to issue financial statements.

The Materiality Principle in Action

Let's imagine that a business suffered from significant damages during a hurricane. After struggling with the insurance company for months, they finally report an extraordinary loss valued at $15,000. For a small business with a net income of just $60,000, this would be 25% of their value and would need to be reported. For a company that has a net income of around $10,000,000, the loss is not considered significant to report.

How to Determine Materiality

Materiality is an accounting principle that requires judgment. Smaller businesses are more likely to list items because of this principle, as their smaller valuation means every asset accounts for a greater percentage of their business. However, a multi-national corporation would have many immaterial items because they account for less of their total assets.

In addition to being applied to monetary events, this can be applied to events of a certain nature. For example, transactions that are personal instead of business should not be recorded. In addition to applying the materiality principle to size, it should be used to consider the nature of the event. For example, imagine that a company operated a casino where new laws were being enacted that would significantly impact the company's operations. This non-material item is something that should be disclosed, as it is going to have a significant impact on the company in the future.

Sometimes, the principle of materiality involves creating estimates. Other times, the principle of materiality means avoiding making an estimate because it may be unreliable to estimate or calculate certain circumstances. In this case, an auditor or accountant may need to create a threshold as an estimate, using a percentage rather than a definitive number.

CHAPTER 12

The Monetary Unit Principle

The monetary unit principle is a regulation for the way a company reports their financial standing to the SEC and their shareholders using a single monetary unit. It is the generally accepted guideline that companies should report their transactions and express them through their monetary value in currency. Additionally, this currency should remain consistent from period to period to align with the consistency principle.

What is the Monetary Unit Principle?

The monetary unit principle is used to establish rules regarding currency and monetary units. First, this principle states that businesses can only record transactions that have financial value. It is not possible (or ethical) to quantify the value of customer service through the company, the creativity of the marketing staff, or the skill levels of different employees. Even though these things may have significant value to the company, there is no way to place a definitive value on them. Without a monetary value, they do not belong on the balance sheet or the financial ledger.

The monetary unit principle also operates using the assumption that currency value remains relatively stable. The principle is flawed slightly in this regard, as many economies are undergoing high inflation rates right now. The purchasing power of the 'dollar' has significantly declined in many economies, so the value of a dollar twenty years ago is not the same as it is today. Currently, however, the FASB does not require companies to report changes of inflation on their financial statements.

Comparisons and the Monetary Unit Principle

Among the benefits of the monetary unit principle is its ability to let financial statements of companies in different countries be compared even when they do not use the same financial unit. When economies are regularly stable, the conversion rate between various currencies also remains stable. This is important for international companies that may have stockholders in different countries, as they can compare the financials of one business to another. If there is one area that seems to be better or worse, then management can review differences in the operation of a company and decide if any actions can be taken to improve the processes that are not as efficient.

Limitations of the Monetary Unit Principle

The biggest limitation of the monetary unit principle is in economies that suffer from hyperinflation. Even though companies in the United States are not yet required to revaluate and adjust all the items on their financial statement, there may be a day when it is necessary to do this to provide an accurate financial picture to investors. This has happened in countries like Brazil and South Africa, as the economy has inflated at a rapid rate. Currently, the FASB is not concerned about this because the United States has had a relatively low inflation rate over time. Should the economy and the value of the dollar begin to inflate or deflate rapidly, however, this principle may change and the monetary unit principle may no longer be applicable.

However, something that is noted is that the monetary unit principle focuses more on inflation from period-to-period, rather than over a period like a decade (or several). As it focuses on short-term assets and creating consistency more in the present time, then there is not as much risk for drastic fluctuations in the values of currency over time.

The Monetary Unit Principle in Action

The monetary unit principle is best displayed as a building that grows in value over time. For example, imagine that a business purchases a building for just $45,000. They make improvements to the building and over time, the neighborhood changes. The value and interest in the neighborhood and economy at the time inflates. As it does, the building is valued at $115,000 instead of the price originally paid for it. Even though the asset is worth significantly more than it was at the time of purchase, the company would not revaluate the building because of the monetary unit principle. This also ties into the cost principle, as the building should be set at the value of its purchase price, rather than its potential value during resale. If the company were to decide to sell the building and make a profit, then they would realize the amount that they received from the sale (and still not the value of the company).

CHAPTER 13

Reliability Principle

A ccounting must be carried out in a way that is reliable, as a company's reliability affects the willingness of lenders, suppliers, creditors, stockholders, and other businesses to do business with them. After all, nobody wants to do business with a company that is considered shady or has its ethics called into question.

The reliability principle is the idea that companies should only record those financial transactions that can be verified. Even cash transactions should be recorded using receipts or a register machine. By choosing to use only verifiable transactions, companies are better able to leave a paper trail for transactions within the company. This is very important should their ethics every be called into question or if an audit is conducted.

What is the Reliability Principle?

The reliability principle or objectivity principle is the accounting practice of only recording transactions you can verify in the accounts. Recorded accounts should be verified with objective evidence, including appraisal reports, bank statements, purchase receipts, promissory notes, and canceled checks. The ideal reports are going to be those generated from outside the company, as any company can create their own receipts and forge a paper trail.

The Reliability Principle and Other Concepts

The reliable principle aligns with many other concepts in accounting, so it should be used regardless of a company's financial standing or other outside events. First, the reliability principle allows all information with neutrality. This is free of any bias that might sway a stockholder or investor. Additionally, it allows for a fair, complete, and accurate view of the way a company is performing. Without all verifiable transactions being included and those that are not verifiable being excluded, it could paint an inaccurate picture of a company's finances. Finally, this aligns with the idea of prudence, which means that caution should be taken when accounting to adhere to all financial principles and be successful in reporting information in a fair, accurate way.

The easiest way for companies to adhere to these principles is to be honest about what happened in their financial period. The same conclusions should be drawn regardless of who is interpreting the statement and all statements should reflect what actually happened during an accounting period.

Acceptable Third-Party Documents

Even though receipts from a company's transactions may be useful, these and other internally-generated documents are not necessarily considered accurate enough for an auditor to use to either prove or disprove appropriate financial reporting activities. This is because internally-generated documents can be created by anyone with a printer and access to computer software.

The preferred evidence of a paper trail for the IRS and SEC is third-party documents, which are documents that offer verification that comes from outside of a company. Rather than relying on what a company says they have done, third-party documents prove that a company had a financial transaction with that other party. Some examples of third-party documents created by other entities include valuation experts, customers, banks, and suppliers. Third-party documents have higher reliability than documents provided by an entity, particularly if there is an audit or their accounting techniques are called into question.

Limitations of the Reliability Principle

One of the biggest challenges new start-ups have is verifying their receipts. This is especially tricky when accepting cash payments for goods or services and if record-keeping is poor. This is especially true because smaller start-ups may not have a lot of credit built with suppliers or lenders. Many small businesses also do not offer stock options in their company until they are ready to grow into a publicly-traded company. Therefore, there is a limited paper trail and bookkeeping may be poor. This can leave a company in trouble if they are audited, especially as the responsibility then falls on them to prove where money has been coming into and going out of the company.

It can also be difficult to create a paper trail and work according to the reliability principle when creating reserve accounts within the company. Reserve accounts are those designed to cushion the financial blow of anticipated problems within a company. They are allowances for debts that will not significantly impact the financial statement. For example, there may be an allowance for unsold inventory that becomes obsolete and cannot be sold at a discounted price. Companies also commonly create an allowance for doubtful accounts, which is an account that offsets the debt caused by customers that do not pay their accounts.

It can also be difficult to use this principle for the retained earnings reserve where the money is usually set to reserve it from being paid as dividends. These are opinion-based, thus, they can be difficult to verify.

The best defense when creating these types of accounts is to include calculations, evident patterns, or plans related to the account being called into question. For example, a company may calculate the average percentage of customers that fail to pay their account each period and use this calculation to justify their amount in the allowance for doubtful accounts account. If they set aside money in retained earnings, they may justify this by including the plans for how the money will be spent and the research on how much the project is going to cost. Basically, companies should not record any financial transaction that cannot be proven or verified in some way. Avoiding unethical recording helps a business maintain its reputation and avoid being called into question by auditors.

CHAPTER 14

Revenue Recognition Principle

The revenue recognition principle exists in accordance with accrual accounting principles, as it requires companies to recognize their revenues in the same period when they are fulfilled, rather than the period when the customer pays for the work. It would be very difficult to create a cause-and-effect relationship without the revenue recognition principle, especially in service industries when the work may be completed at one time and the amount owed may be due later.

What is the Revenue Recognition Principle?

This is the principle that companies should recognize revenue upon completion of a job (usually when an invoice is sent out or service is completed), rather than recognizing it when the payment is collected. For example, if a lawn mowing company charges a standard fee of $70 to mow a church's lawn, they would recognize the earnings when the lawn is mowed instead of waiting for the church to pay for the service. The revenue recognition principle is recognized when using accrual basis accounting, but not when using cash basis accounting.

When an entry is made in the financial accounts, it represents a company's entitlement to receiving that amount. This is the reason it is often recorded in accounts receivable, with the exception of cash payments that are paid upon the delivery of goods or services. Of course, the transaction must be able to be communicated in monetary value for the information to be included in the financial statements. Additionally, it is required that companies prove they are going to recognize this revenue. This may be one of the reasons that businesses do not realize revenue until they have already completed the service. They must first send the invoice or another document that proves the sale, then they can record it in accordance with both the revenue recognition principle and the reliability principle.

Updates to the Revenue Recognition Principle

The FASB changed the rules of the revenue recognition principle as recently as 2014 when it was realized the old principle was unclear and left room for error when financial statements were being prepared.

The FASB issued five steps that allow every company to consistently and accurately recognize revenue in its financial statements. The first step is establishing a contract between the entity and the customer. After the contract is identified, the company identifies what obligations they must perform to fulfill the contract. Next, the transaction price is determined. A link is created between the transaction price and the obligations that must be fulfilled to earn that revenue. When the performance obligations are completed, the revenue is recognized. In accordance with the matching principle, the organization reports any expenses incurred while realizing this revenue at the same time.

By establishing a new core for revenue recognition, the FASB hopes to overcome some of their current problems with financial reporting and make it easier to establish an industry standard that lets revenue be compared from different companies, regardless of their own methods of reporting. By using a single model, every company is likely to report revenue in the same way. This is especially true in service industries, such as those helping build or implement software, marketing agencies, and countless others.

Using the Revenue Recognition Principle for Goods or Services

The sale of goods is slightly different than the sale of services, especially for small start-ups that might only do customer transactions inside the store. When a company sells goods, they must be able to measure goods sold reliably. Then, this amount can be considered an inflow into the company and the associated expenses can be measured and recorded. Of course, for goods to be recorded under the revenue recognition principle, there should be no risks and rewards with the transaction. The goods must be transferred from the business to the customer and under no circumstances should a company realize revenue for goods that they still maintain some control over.

When rendering services, criteria for the revenue recognition principle states that a business must be able to accurately measure a service's value, as well as any costs related to providing that service. This establishes the probability of inflow of revenue into the business. In addition to measuring the service and costs, some areas require that a company use the stage of completion method for revenue recognition. For this method to be used, it must be the most accurate and honest portrayal of a company's cash inflow. A company must also be able to reliably measure the stage of completion that a project is at before being able to assign a value to it.

Limitations of the Revenue Recognition Principle

Of course, the biggest risk when a company recognizes revenue before it is collected is that the customer will not pay the account. Usually, companies calculate an allowance for doubtful accounts based on the average percentage of customers that do not pay for their goods or services.

One exception of this is when a payment is received in advance. For this to work using this method, an entity would record any revenue paid in advance for the service as a liability. Once the service has been performed, the company is no longer in debt and they can recognize that revenue. For example, if the church pays in advance for three months, the company would recognize it as a liability until the church lawn has been mowed for the three months that were paid for.

Additionally, the exception to the revenue recognition principle is the allowance made for large-scale construction companies. Construction companies use methods to account for the ongoing recognition of revenue and expenses when they are completing long-term projects. This works best for construction companies because they realize gain and loss in every period, especially when they have long-term contracts where it takes months (or longer) to finish providing the service.

The percentage of completion method can only be used by businesses capable of creating accurate estimates for the remaining costs of completion, as well as for how much of the project has been completed when the revenue is recognized. Additionally, the percentage of completion and revenue should also reflect the percentage of estimated expenses that have already been used up (and those that will be needed) as an estimate.

To remain in accordance with both the revenue recognition principle and the reliability principle, a company must include its reasonable calculations as a supplement when creating financial statements or when providing information for an audit. This and any paperwork related to the contract allows the company to create dependable estimates for using this method. There are several methods used in conjunction with the percentage of completion method, depending on which one can satisfy the proper conditions for revenue to be realized. These include:

- Units-of-Delivery Method- The unit of delivery method works best for long-term contracts where companies may provide services over a period of time. For example, a construction company that is working on building several condos in an area might break the work (and contract) up according to completion of each building and realize revenue (and related expenses) before moving on to the next. Here, they would measure the percentage of work delivered to the buyer's specifications and then record the contract price of the number of units delivered and the expenses that have been reasonably allocated to those specific units.

- Cost-to-Cost Method- This method allows expenses to be matched by revenues, even when the materials have already been purchased. The cost of items not used or installed should not be included when recording financials. Instead, businesses must determine the specific percentage of work completed and relate associated costs with that amount of work. This method works well for job-specific machinery that may be bought, provided the company retains the title. The cost of the machinery should be recorded over the lifetime of the asset, even if the lifetime of the asset only spans over the completion of a single long-term contract.

- Efforts-Expended Method- This method accounts for the machine hours, materials used, or direct labor hours when fulfilling a service. For example, a company might realize that it is going to take 5,000 labor hours to complete a project. They might use the number of labor hours completed to determine how much of the project has been completed. For example, if the team puts in 500 cumulative hours by the end of the week, they might account for 10% of the project being completed when they record revenue and expenses.

CHAPTER 15

The Time Period Principle

Consistency is an important element when reporting financial information. Without consistency, it would be impossible to compare one period to the next. For example, imagine that a company releases two statements; one weekly and one monthly. You could not use these two statements to calculate ratios or compare the two financial statements in any way and expect to get an accurate representation of the company's financial standings. The time period assumption exists to ensure businesses report in a consistent manner and in accordance with recognized financial periods. Even though they may create internal reports monthly (or even weekly in some cases), most companies are required to provide financial statements at least once per year. Often, they help customers keep track of their earnings by reporting quarterly as well, which is approximately every three months.

What is the Time Period Principle?

The time period principle describes different reporting periods for a business, usually over a standard period of time. Financial results are usually reported monthly, quarterly, or annually, though a combination of these is usually used. Monthly are most common for internal reports, as these help business owners make decisions about how to best allocate resources and notice possible problems and trends. This principle is also known as the periodicity assumption.

The periods describe a certain time within a business. A business' periodicity is divided into accounting periods for its entire lifetime, usually into accounting periods with the same length. When creating a financial statement, a header is included that describes the time period. Statements should also include dates. When choosing which financial transactions to include, as well as which revenues and expenses should be realized, all the information included on and pertaining to that financial statement should fall within the dates mentioned at the top of the statement.

Why is the Time Period Principle Important?

In addition to establishing a consistent period of time for financial analysis, the time period principle allows companies to take an accurate screenshot of their financial standings. With time periods, businesses can recognize revenue and expenses as they are incurred by period.

The time period principle is one applied to all areas of accounting. Even companies using the cash-basis method of accounting will need to use this principle to create segments of time in their business. Then, finances can be reported in these periods.

Frequency of Reports and the Fiscal Year

In most cases, companies generate external reports at least once annually. In this case, the accounting period lasts 12 months. Some companies choose to begin their year on January 1 and end on December 31. For others, a fiscal accounting year is used. This can be any day, as long as it is an annual period. For example, a company might release its financial statements from March 1 of one year to February 2 of the next. Accounting reports are released more frequently when a timely report is needed.

The fiscal year is ideal for companies that experience high levels of sales during the holidays, such as retail locations or jewelers. Companies may also choose their financial fiscal year depending on the official start date of their company. Time periods can be thought of as artificial, as there is no specific guideline for which dates a company must use to report.

The decision on how to use periodicity is usually made at the start of a company. They must decide if they are going to report their revenue as is and report for a partial year (such as a company that begins their startup in May or June) or if they are going to report using a fiscal period. Even though some companies opt for a fiscal period, they may choose to do this using dates that are near those when taxes are due. Otherwise, they would end preparing separate financial statements when filing taxes and when reporting to other external parties, which is not a good use of company time.

The Time Period Principle and Other Principles

For the matching principle and the revenue recognition principle to be followed, companies must be able to have time periods to match their revenues and expenses to. Otherwise, the matching of revenues and expenses would be irrelevant and immeasurable. Not to mention, without the time period principle, trying to report any kind of financial information would be messy, unverifiable, and unreliable.

The time period principle is also closely related to the going concern principle. As businesses operate as if they are going to remain in business, they can accrue accounts payable and accounts receivable. This gives flexibility when reporting, while still adhering to the time period principle and the principles of revenue recognition and matching.

CHAPTER 16

Applying the Principles of Accounting to the Accounting Cycle

Before financial statements can be completed, all the information needs to be collected and put together in the right way. The accounting cycle can be broken down into 9 steps that make the entire process a lot less intimidating. Now that you are familiar with the principles of accounting, you should be able to apply them to the accounting cycle for preparing statements and analyzing financial data.

Step 1: Identification and Analysis of Business Transactions

Accountants first go through all the business transactions and events that have occurred since the last reporting cycle. It's important that the transactions pertaining to the business entity are separated from those that do not. When good records are kept and the business owners keep their personal finances separate from the finances of the business, it is significantly easier to do this first step.

Once all the appropriate receipts are separated from those not pertaining to the business, the transactions are analyzed. They should be organized according to date, as this will make the next process easier. While analyzing, you must decide which accounts to debit and which accounts to credit. Though you are going to copy these amounts in the journals, you should keep the primary information as source documents. In the case of a discrepancy or an audit, the source documents are considered more reliable than prepared financial statements or journal entries.

Step 2: Journal Entries

Next, you are going to record the source documents in the journals. The double-entry accounting method is used, so every journal entry is going to include the date, a description, and at least two accounts. One account will be a debit and the other will be a credit. Something to note is that it is possible to have more than two accounts for a single journal entry. For example, if a company has paid part of their rent in advance, the entry might look like this:

Jan 17	Rent Expense	4500	
	Cash		2700
	Rent Payable		1800

A basic entry that has just two entries might look like:

Aug 11	Cost of Maintenance and Repairs	675	
	Cash		675

As journals are the first official recording of business transactions, they are often called the Books of Original Entry.

Accounts You Will Use When Writing Journal Entries

As you create journal entries, the biggest challenge is going to be deciding which accounts to debit and which accounts to credit. Accounts are classified according to a specified account. For example, assets are usually broken down into four categories; current assets, long-term assets, prepaid and deferred assets, and intangible assets.

These are the accounts most commonly listed on the income statement:

Revenue

- Sales

Cost of Goods Sold

- Cost of Goods Sold

Operating Expenses

- Salaries and Wages

- Marketing Expense

- Advertising Expense

- Rent Expense

- Insurance Expense

- Amortization Expense

- Utilities Expense

Other Income

- Interest Income

- Gain on Sale

Other Expenses

- Interest Expense

- Loss on Sale

Income Tax

- Taxes

These are the accounts most commonly listed on the balance sheet:

Current Assets

- Cash

- Inventory

- Accounts Receivable

- Prepaid Expenses

- Marketable Securities

- Allowance for Doubtful Accounts

Fixed Assets

- Land

- Equipment

- Buildings

- Accumulated Depreciation

- Leasehold Improvements

Intangible Assets

- Intellectual Property

- Goodwill

Investments

- Investments in Stocks

- Investments in Bonds

Current Liability

- Accounts Payable

- Income Tax Payable

- Cash Dividends Payable

Shareholders Equity

- Common Stock

- Capital Stock

- Preferred Stock

- Treasury Stock

- Dividends

- Retained Earnings

- Paid-In Capital

Another Note About Journal Entries

Writing journal entries can be compared to Newton's third law of motion. Every action should have an opposite and equal reaction. This means two things. First, you should expect that every journal entry requires at least two entries. Second, you should expect that your two journal entries equate to the same amount.

In the case of needing more than one journal entry, two of the entries will have the same value in either debits or credits as the other entry has in debits or credits. This creates a balance that is necessary for checking company financials and being sure that all the values align properly.

The reason balance is so important is because it verifies a company's earnings. It prevents employees and business owners from stealing from the company, a practice which is called embezzlement. There have been many cases of embezzlement, though the numbers eventually failed to add up and the responsible party was held accountable for their actions.

Bernie Madoff is a famous investor who was arrested in 2008 after a complex scheme allowed him to convince investors to give him $65 billion that he stole from the company. He was sentenced to 150 years in prison. He was charged with false filings, investment advisor fraud, securities fraud, and money laundering with 11 total charges brought against him.

Kenneth Lay was the CEO of Enron who is known for his role in the bankruptcy of the natural gas company. After years of accounting fraud and corporate abuse, Lay cost shareholders of Enron close to $11 billion. Though he was charged, Lay died before sentencing.

There are countless other examples of fraud and embezzlement throughout larger companies. Though many forged accounting statements for some time, the truth eventually came to light and the people responsible in these cases were punished severely. In a way, being aware of discrepancies when the books just do not add up can help uncover these schemes, particularly when whoever is stealing from the company does not fully cover their tracks.

Examples of Journal Entries

Once you are following the rule of equal and opposite reactions, the biggest obstacle is going to be deciding which accounts to debit/credit with transactions. The best way to do this is through practice. Don't worry if it takes time, you'll get the hang of it eventually. Something else that is useful is recording what each entry is for. This makes it simpler to track the flow of cash, particularly if you find yourself unbalanced later. As you create the journal entries, note what each entry stands for. The ideal entry is going to look like this:

Date	Account Name	Debit	Credit
June 12			
	Supplies Expense	500	
	Cash		500
	To record the purchase of supplies		

As you can see, each entry is going to include the date, which accounts are involved in the transaction, the debits and credits associated with the transaction, and information about the transaction. Here are a few examples you can look over to get some ideas about how to create a journal entry.

Scenario 1: Purchasing Inventory

Imagine that a company purchased inventory with a total cost of $75,000. They paid $15,000 on delivery and will be invoiced for the remaining amount.

The inventory account would be debited 75,000, which represents the total amount of inventory gained. The cash account would be credited the 15,000 that was paid, while the accounts payable account would be credited the remaining 60,000 that they owe to the other company.

Scenario 2- Purchase of Equipment

If a company has a transaction that involves only cash, it is rather simple. If a company buys a computer system worth $15,000 and pays it in cash, the equipment account would be debited 15,000 and the cash account would be credited 15,000.

Scenario 3- A vendor payment is due

When a company agrees to exchange the goods or services of another company for cash, they are typically invoiced later. Before the due date, the amount is assigned to accounts payable. It is a liability for which the company is responsible for. For example, the payment of materials amounting to $4,000 would debit the supplies account and credit the accounts payable account. Once the inventory payment is due, accounts payable is debited $4,000 and cash is credited $4,000.

Scenario 4- Borrowing money from the bank

This is a simple journal entry in most cases, though it can be confusing if there is an additional amount of interest on the loan. If a company borrowed $20,000 from the bank, they would debit the cash account 20,000 and credit the bank loan payable account 20,000. If they owed $100 interest on this amount, a second entry would be made. The 100 interest would be debited to the interest expense account and credited to accounts payable or interest payable.

Scenario 5- Acquiring land and building for a factory

Imagine that a company made a $310,000 purchase, $110,000 for a piece of land and $200,000 for the building sitting on it. They paid $50,000 of this amount up front and the rest will be owed in the future. To create this journal entry, land would be debited 110,000 and buildings would be debited 200,000. The 50,000 cash paid would be credited to the cash account and the remaining 260,000 would be credited to notes payable. The debit of the land and buildings is equivalent to the credits to cash and note payable.

Scenario 6: Recording the sale of inventory

A store sells a violin for $800 that cost the company $150 to manufacture. They would debit the cash account 800 to account for the sale and the cost of goods sold account $150 to reflect the amount deducted for the production of the violin. Then, the revenue account is credited $800 for the sale and the inventory account is decreased by the amount it took to manufacture the violin, or 150.

Scenario 7- Employees are paid

For this scenario, the total amount of wages is tracked per wage period. For this reason, this transaction may appear more than once per cycle. To record employee's being paid a total of $4,524 in wages, the entry would debit the wages expense and credit the cash account.

Scenario 8- A business owner enters a contract where he will pay $700 monthly for an office space

This is a tricky scenario. When a lease is signed, even though the business owner is entering an agreement, no cash is changing hands. There are no expenses and the company cannot recognize any revenue from using that space. As a result, there is no journal entry to record entering a rental lease.

Step 3: Posting Entries to the Ledger

The ledger is used to aggregate the different accounts and provide an overall amount for each of them. This helps accountants reach a total amount that can be debited or credited to the ledger. For example, you would go through each page of the journal and add all the cash debits and cash credits. In the end, the difference of cash credits and debits would be either debited or credited to the accounts on the ledger (depending on if the credits or debits are larger). This is done for all the accounts.

One of the most common ways of preparing the ledger from the journal entries is T accounts. To do this, you'll need a T account for each account you use when creating journal entries and preparing your balance sheet. The T account is simply an entry that is headed using the proper account that has two columns. It is called a T account because of the shape of the entry.

To create a T account, simply place all the debits on the left-hand side of the 'T" and all the credits on the right-hand side of the

"T". The position of values on the T account will be determined by whether they are a positive or negative value, or a debit or credit. For assets, the debits will be positive amounts and the credits will be negative amounts. For both liability and equity, the debits will be negative amounts and the credits will be positive amounts. This makes sense, as all the debits (positives) from the debit column of assets will equal the positive value of the credits in liability and equity. Likewise, all the negative credits associated with assets will be the same amount as the negative credits of equity and liability.

Step 4: Creating the Unadjusted Trial Balance

The purpose of a balance sheet is to have the same number of debits and credits. This is a sign that a company has credited and debited the proper accounts for each transaction. To create a trial balance, add all the credits from the ledger in one column and add all the debits in the other. The two amounts should be the same if the entries are correct.

The purpose of a trial balance is to determine if there are any errors. If there are errors, they'll need to be reversed or rectified and you'll move on to the next step. Here's an example of what an unadjusted trial balance might look like:

Cash	21,690	
Accounts Receivable	6,100	
Office Supplies	18,900	
Prepaid Rent	24,000	
Equipment	95,000	
Accounts Payable		6,200
Notes Payable		35,000
Utilities Payable		2,490
Unearned Revenue		4,300
Common Stock		100,000
Service Revenue		65,300
Wages Expense	34,900	
Miscellaneous Expense	4,200	
Electricity Expense	2,400	
Telephone Expense	1,500	
Dividend	4,600	
Total	**213,290**	**213,290**

Step 5: Adjusting Entries

Adjusting entries are those that have not yet been recorded between the preparation of the financial statement and the official reporting of the statement. There may also be some income that has been earned without being entered into the ledgers.

These adjustments are posted to the accounts before the summary. You may have to adjust some of the amounts in the trial balance to reflect the new numbers. Usually, adjustments are used to report prepayments, allowances, depreciation, deferrals, accrual of income, and accrual of expenses.

For example, an asset with a present cash value of $13,000 with a depreciation of $400 per month would be adjusted at this time. The entry might look like this:

Sep 13			
	Depreciation	400	
	Accumulated Depreciation		400
	To record scheduled depreciation		

This is also the time when a company accounts for those things changed by adhering to the accrual accounting principle. For example, imagine that a company was prepaid $900 for providing a service. In the initial recording entry, the company would have debited the cash account and credited the unearned revenue account. Once they have completed the work, the adjusting entry would debit the unearned revenue account 900 and credit the sales revenue account.

On the opposite side, when a company sends an invoice for work completed that can be paid the following month, the accounts receivable account is debited and the sales revenue account is credited.

Step 6: Adjusted Trial Balance

An adjusted trial balance takes the adjusting entries into account and debits or credits them to the accounts on the unadjusted trial balance. When you add the debits and credits, they should equal the same number. If you cannot reach a balanced state, you'll likely need to go over your work and see where you went wrong.

Another example would be the adjustment entry made for employee wages that were accrued in one period and paid in another. The initial entry would debit wages expense and credit wages payable. The adjusting entry would debit wages payable and credit the cash account.

Step 7: Financial Statements

Once the accounts are up-to-date and you have checked the math, you can prepare the financial statements. If you are creating a complete set of statements, you'll need to include the statement of comprehensive income, statement of changes in equity, balance sheet, statement of cash flows, and notes to financial statements.

There are five base elements to all the financial statements, including assets, liabilities, equity, income, and expense. By analyzing companies in these areas, it gives a broad scope of the finances of the company without going into the finer details that most investors and stockholders are not interested in.

Within the accounting statements, income is meant to describe any economic benefits. This includes inflowing cash or the improvement of an asset, however, it also can be the decrease in liabilities or amounts owed. What is not included in income is any equity derived from shareholders, as this amount does not reflect money earned by the company using its resources to generate revenue.

Put simply, revenue is that tracking of a company's revenue and gains. Revenue is any money that arises from normal business proceedings. For a private tutor, the revenue would be the cost of a session paid as their fee. For a furniture manufacturer, revenue would come from the sale of furniture. Gain, by contrast, represents money that a company has earned outside their normal scope of business. If a furniture manufacturer decided to sell one of their machines after replacing it with a new one, they could realize any amount earned on the old asset as a gain.

Expenses are any decrease in the economic benefits realized by the business. This includes money spent on operating expenses as well as the deterioration of an asset. Expenses could also be increases to a company's liabilities. The information that is excluded is any outflow or distribution to shareholders, as this is also considered equity. In addition to including expenses, the expenses are included as losses of the business. For example, if the furniture manufacturer sold their machine asset at a lower price than its depreciable cost, it would result in a loss that would be recognized as an expense.

There is also an additional area of the financial statements where equity is discussed. Equity is the money that an entity can use to make changes, invest in activities, and use to generate revenue. However, this equity is not considered part of a company's normal profits and losses because it is not related to doing business. Equity includes stock that has been issued and contributions from the owners into the company. When a company experiences a gain, they often decide how much to put back into the business and how much they will distribute to stockholders and owners to maintain their line of equity.

The Statement of Comprehensive Income

The statement of comprehensive income and the balance sheet are two similar statements as they both reflect an entity's financial position. The major difference is that the statement of comprehensive income tracks the performance across a period of time, while the balance sheet displays the performance at a given day.

This comparison is made by analyzing income and revenue with expenses and costs. When the income exceeds the expenses, then a company is generating a gain in income. When the expenses are greater than the income, the entity is facing losses. It is not uncommon for entities to face losses in some periods, especially if hard times have fallen on the business or they go through a period of fewer sales. However, by revisiting strategies and having enough in reserves to cover expenses during these times, a business can ensure its longevity and success.

Information about profit and loss, as well as equity, is reported in different parts of the comprehensive income statement. The financial standings of many companies would be vastly different without contributions from owners and stakeholders, especially once a company has expanded and requires more capital to finance more revenue in the future. While both pieces of information are important, they are not relevant to each other and are included in different areas of the financial statements.

Items pertaining to profit or loss are reported in the comprehensive income statement. The income statement should report only on the income and expenses, excluding any items that should be reported in Other Comprehensive Income Statement. It is in the other comprehensive income statement that items affecting owners equity and shareholders equity are reported. This includes any information affecting the overall value of a company that cannot be considered a profit or a loss. These two statements are either kept separately or reported together, with the comprehensive income statement being in part one of a financial report and the other comprehensive income statement being in part two. Here's an example of what a comprehensive income statement is going to look like, with both parts of the statement included as separate (but related) documents. This imaginary company is a music shop that sells instruments and also offers lessons.

Music Shop

Income Statement

For the Year Ended January 31, 2012

Revenues		
Merchandise Sales	32,750	
Lesson Income	15,900	
Total Revenues:		48,650
Expenses		
Cost of Goods Sold	7,910	
Depreciation Expense	400	
Wage Expense	5,700	
Interest Expense	240	
Supplies Expense	3,040	
Rent Expense	1,600	
Utilities Expense	510	
Total Expenses:		18, 400
Net Income		**30,250**

Music Shop
Comprehensive Income Statement
For the Year Ended January 31, 2012

Net Income		30,250
Other Comprehensive Income		
Unrealized gain on securities for sale	1,400	
Unrealized loss on securities held to maturity	(less) 510	
Foreign currency adjustments	(less)450	440
Comprehensive Income		30,690

Statement of Changes in Equity

The statement of changes in equity is used to help shareholders and owners track the equity within a company, which is the most relevant to paying out dividends. The information needed for this statement include:

- Net profit or loss that pertains to shareholders

- Increase or decrease of shared capital reserves

- Gains and losses that directly effect equity (such as one of the owners withdrawing capital)

- Effects of corrections from errors in the previous period

- Effects of changes in accounting policies

- Dividend payments to shareholders

The statement of changes in equity is important because it displays information about a company's equity in greater detail than any of the other statements. Here's an example of what the statement of changes in equity for ABC company might look like:

ABC Company
Statement of changes in equity for the year ended 31st December 2010

	Share Capital	Retained Earnings	Revaluation Surplus	Total Equity
Balance at 1 January 2009	150,000	35,000	-	185,000
Changes in accounting policy	-	-	-	-
Correction of prior period error	-	-	-	-
Restated balance	150,000	35,000	-	185,000
Changes in equity for the year 2009				
Issue of share capital	-	-	-	-
Income for the year	-	30,000	-	30,000
Revaluation gain	-	-	10,000	10,000
Dividends	-	(20,000)		(20,000)
Balance at 31 December 2010	150,000	45,000	10,000	205,000

The opening balance reflected at the beginning of the statement is meant to give stakeholders a clear picture of where each of the accounts was sitting at the beginning of the period that the current period is being compared to. This is an unadjusted balance, as it should not include any effects from changes in accounting policy or errors from the previous period. Below this, the effect of changes in accounting policy and the effect of correction of prior period error are included to give an adjusted (and accurate) balance of the revenue at the end of the period. Then, the proper balance for these accounts is restated as amounts from the beginning of the accounting period.

Share capital can be redeemed or purchased during the period, which reflects changes in equity. There are two numbers reported for these changes—the changes in share premium reserve and the changes in share capital reserve. Redemption is deducted, while issued shares increase share capital.

Any dividends that were announced or issued for the period are deducted from shareholder equity in accordance with accrual accounting methods. The wealth distributed to stockholders is being given away and is no longer in the company. Then, the income or loss is reported as it appears on the income statement, as this affects the amount of capital available in the company.

If there were in changes in the revaluation reserve, these would be calculated. The revaluation describes changes in equity realized outside of the income statement. It should be incorporated only if it has not been accounted for in the income statement. Gains and losses are also recognized, however, these must be gains and losses not yet accounted for in the income statement. After the numbers are totaled, the closing balance represents the total amount of money in each account.

The Balance Sheet

The balance sheet is also referred to as the statement of the financial period, as it provides the closest look a company's financial standings. As it does not track the changes from the beginning of a period to the end of the period, it is considered a snapshot of a company's standings at a given moment in time. The balance sheet is used the most by accountants and business owners, though creditors may also use it to see what assets a company has on hand and determine their qualification for loans or lines of credit.

The balance sheet has three categories; assets, liabilities, and owner's (stockholders' equity). Asset accounts include those like cash, petty cash, accounts receivable, temporary investments, prepaid insurance, inventory, supplies, buildings, equipment, land, land improvements, and goodwill. Usually, these accounts have debits when they are considered assets. There are also contra-asset accounts that are listed. Contra assets are those that have credit balances. They are called contra assets because having a credit balance in these areas is contrary to the usual practice of keeping a debit balance. Some examples of contra accounts include accumulated depreciation, accumulated amortization, and allowance for doubtful accounts.

Liabilities commonly have the word 'payable' at the end of the account. In accordance with accrual accounting, liabilities are tracked and accumulated before they are paid for. They represent debts that a company owes in the future. By classifying liabilities, companies can take a closer look at the sources of their funding and if they are using their resources to the best of their ability.

It is generally preferred that companies allow their liabilities to accumulate until they are due since they can use their capital before the balances are due to put back into the company. Companies also record payments that are received before their contract or service is fulfilled as a liability, as they still have to use the resources to fulfill that contract in accordance with the matching principle. Liability accounts typically have credit balances, as they represent future outflows of cash. Some common liability accounts include accounts payable, notes payable, wages payable, salaries payable, interest payable, income taxes payable, lawsuits payable, bonds payable, other accrued expenses payable, warranty liability, customer deposits, and unearned revenues.

Like with asset accounts, there are also contra-liability accounts that generally have a positive balance. Some common accounts listed here include bond issue costs, debt issue costs, discounts on bonds payable, and discount on notes payable.

The equity area of the balance sheet is what brings it to a balanced state. Technically, money in the owner's equity section is money that does not necessarily belong to the company. It has been invested, which generally means the company is granted to use it for a certain amount of time. This can include funds invested by owners and partners. In a publicly traded corporation, the amount in the equity may belong to owners and stockholders, with some owners having invested capital and others having preferred stock. It is not uncommon for publicly-traded companies to offer common stock and preferred stock options, with preferred stock generally being reserved for owners and employees. Some other accounts you may see listed include paid-in capital from treasury stock, paid-in capital in excess of par value, retained earnings, and accumulated other comprehensive income.

The total equity of a company is calculated by subtracting the total amount of liabilities from the total amount of assets. Additionally, by adding the liabilities and owner's equity, you can find the total amount of assets in the company. This is possible because principles like the revenue recognition principle and the matching principle allow the accounts to balance out. The total amount of assets in the company is the total amount of their debts, which is the liabilities and the owner's equity. These formulas allow the balance sheet to balance. Here's an example of what the balance sheet of a publicly traded corporation, Nature Goods, would look like.

Nature Goods

Balance Sheet

December 31, 2015

Assets		Liabilities	
Current assets		Current liabilities	
Cash	3,000	Accounts Payable	34,200
Petty Cash	200	Notes Payable	4,800
Temporary Investments	11,000	Wages Payable	9,000
Accounts Receivable – net	40,200	Interest Payable	1,900
Inventory	45,100	Taxes Payable	6,500
Supplies	4,100	Warranty Liability	1,200
Prepaid Insurance	1,600	Unearned Revenues	2,300
Total Current Assets	**105,200**	Total Current Liabilities	**59,900**
Investments	**33,000**	Long-Term Liabilities	
Property, Plant, & Equipment		Notes Payable	23,000
Land	6,500	Bonds Payable	520,000
Land Improvements	3,400	Total Long-Term Liabilities	**543,000**

Buildings	165,000		
Equipment	204,000		
Less: accum depreciation	65,000	Total Liabilities	**602,900**
Prop, Plant, & Equipment - net	**313,900**		
Intangible Assets		**Stockholder's Equity**	
Goodwill	120,000	Common Stock	115,000
Trade Names	200,000	Retained Earnings	150,000
Total Intangible Assets	**320,000**	Accum Other Comprehensive Income	5000
		Less: Treasury Stock	(100,000)
Other Assets	**4,800**	Total Stockholders' Equity	**170,000**
Total Assets	**772,900**	**Total Liabilities & Stockholders' Equity**	**772,900**

The first two columns are the first part of the balance sheet where all assets are added. Once these numbers are totaled, they should have the same value as the liabilities and equity that are listed in the third and fourth columns.

Statement of Cash Flows

The statement of cash flows is representative of an entire period, rather than just giving a snapshot. It tracks specific changes in the inflow and outflow of cash over the course of the year. Since it is a statement that tracks change, you'll need at least two years worth of financial data to complete this. Generally, the statement of cash flows is completed using the balance sheet from the current year and the previous year, which is the reason this is prepared after the balance sheet. The statement of cash flows also uses information about net income (or loss) and depreciation, which can be found on the income statement. Therefore, this is completed last to help the process go smoother.

Companies can choose one of two methods for preparing their cash flows statement, with both methods being accepted by the FASB. The FASB does have a preference for the direct method, which lists cash receipts from operations, as well as cash disbursements related to those operations. Most companies prefer the simpler indirect method, which begins with the net income from the income statement and then gets adjusted to account for noncash items like depreciation.

The statement of cash flows classifies items according to where they are coming from—operating, investing, or financing activities. Cash flow from operating activities includes accounts like accounts receivable, inventory, and prepaid expenses, which are all directly related to doing business. Cash flow from investing activities includes long-term investments that a business has made in the hopes of realizing more revenue in the future. For example, they might increase the amount spent on assets like machinery in the hopes they will be able to realize more profits in the future. Cash flow from financing activities includes loans from banks and dividends paid out to investors, which help finance the business and allow it to make more investments.

All three of these areas are combined to find the figure for net cash flow. This can be a positive or negative number that represents how a company's cash increases or decreases over the course of a year. Now, let's look at a sample of a cash flows statement for LMN company.

LMN Company

Statement of Cash Flows

For the Period Ending January 31, 2018

Net Income	120,900
Depreciation	55,000
Inc. in Accounts Receivable	(25,000)
Inc. in Inventory	(13,000)
Dec. in Prepaid Expenses	8,000
Inc. in Accounts Payable	35,000
Dec. in Accruals	(6,000)
Net Cash Flows from Operating Activities	**174,900**
Inc. in Investments	(25,000)
Inc. in Plant & Equipment	(110,000)
Net Cash Flows from Investment Activities	**(135,000)**
Inc. in Bank Loans	60,000
Dividends Paid	(55,000)
Net Cash Flows from Financing Activities	**5000**
Net Increase in Cash Flows	**44,900**

You may have noticed some areas of the cash flow statements are a little confusing. For example, how could an increase in accounts receivable be considered a negative amount? When a company allows a customer to purchase their goods on credit, they have less money in the current moment. The same is true of increases in plant and equipment. Likewise, even though the bank loans are something that increases a company's eventual debt, it increases cash flow at the present moment and thus is considered a positive financial event. The statement of cash flows involves the amount of cash flowing in and out of the company. When they have less working capital, there is less money to invest with.

Notes to the Financial Statements

Businesses can technically include any information they find relevant to the financial statements and their interpretations when they are creating to the notes to the financial statements. The notes to the financial statements are explanatory notes that offer more information about the company. This is a time for businesses to disclose anything they may find important. As all businesses are unique and go through different situational circumstances that may require disclosure in the financial statements, it can be hard to decide which items to include. As a general principle, accountants should follow the principles of full disclosure and materiality when adding their notes. Even though they should disclose information that has impacted the financial standing of the company in a significant way, they do not have to worry about every minute detail that has affected their finances. Smaller businesses are more likely to need to report key items, as they have a lower net worth and will be affected more significantly than a larger business. Here are some of the information that may be disclosed in the notes to the financial statements:

- Notes reflecting the basis of the company's presentation- Some businesses operate by creating a contract and providing a service. Others manufacture goods and sell them. There are even businesses that purchase goods and then sell them to customers to realize a profit. Companies may disclose their inner workings of the business by quickly describing their process of generating revenue from their operations.

- Advisements on important accounting practices- Even though the GAAP exists to create some consistency in accounting practices, this does not mean that companies all have to follow the same strategies. There is wiggle room for companies to choose how to use these principles appropriately when reporting the financials of their business. For this reason, they may disclose some of the key principles they follow and the overall effects on the financial statement, as this gives a fairer presentation of the statements. Some information that might be included is their method for accounting for intangibles, how taxes are accounted for, the method of depreciation being used, benefits offered to employees, and how the company values its inventory.

- Disclosure of subsequent events- Sometimes, companies are aware of a significant event before it happens. Even once the accounting period is over, it may be necessary to disclose known events that are going to happen. Of course, the materiality principle is in play here as well because not all events need to be reported.

- Information on intangible assets- Many company's place value on their intangible assets, though the direct benefits can never be realized. Companies may include information on how they have chosen to valuate their intangible assets and how they arrived at the number displayed on the balance sheet.

- Notes revealing contingencies- Contingent liabilities are losses that are not yet realized, but that have a potential of happening. For example, imagine that a company was in the process of being audited by the IRS for the first year of their revenue, which included some of the owner's personal transactions as transactions from within the business. More than likely, this dispute is going to result in a fine. Companies would disclose this contingency if it was believed that it may happen and if it would make a significant change in the financial standing of the company, as fines and settling debts from erroneous tax forms can cost a company tens of thousands of dollars.

- Debt Recording Notes- This is where companies note any claims that creditors may have against their company and the period in which these claims will be due. If a company leans too much on creditors, it can cover up significant amounts of debt but they may find themselves drowning when it is time to pay the loan back. Including this information is important because failing to include it skews the appearance of the company's financial standing.

Step 8: Closing Entries

Entities close out temporary accounts to get ready for the next accounting period. For example, income and expense accounts for the month will be zeroed out so they can be accurately calculated the next month. Usually, these are closed using a summary account. The goal of closing entries is to remove those temporary accounts that a company uses to help keep track of earnings during the financial period.

When accounts are closed, only revenue, expense, and dividend accounts are closed. These accounts fluctuate depending on the money coming into and going out of the company. The asset, liability, common stock, and retained earnings accounts are not closed. By zeroing out the temporary accounts, a company has a clean slate and can appropriately track its earnings for the next period.

The first step is to close the revenue account. The amount listed here is transferred as a credit to the income summary account. The income summary account allows information to be recorded before the accounts are closed. Next, the expenses are transferred as debits to the income summary account. Once all this is transferred, the difference between the revenue and expenses is calculated. The income summary account is closed by transferring this amount to the retained earnings account. The amount for the dividends account should also be transferred as a debit to the retained earnings account.

Step 9: Post-Closing Trial Balance

Once closing entries are made, the debits and credits should be balanced again to check accuracy. Only real accounts can be balanced, meaning those accounts that begin with a balance from the previous accounting period. Real accounts are also considered permanent accounts. Some of the real accounts on the balance sheet include assets, liabilities, and stockholders' equity. All the accounts that were closed out in the last step are not included. Here's a look of what company DEF's post-closing trial balance might look like:

Company DEF

Post-Closing Adjusted Trial Balance

For the Period Ending December 31, 2003

	Debit	**Credit**
Cash	25,180	-
Accounts Receivable	4,500	-
Office Supplies	5,100	-
Prepaid Rent	25,000	-
Equipment	100,000	-
Accounts Payable	-	19,200
Utilities Payable	-	3,200
Unearned Revenue	-	4,100
Interest Payable	-	200
Notes Payable	-	15,000
Common Stock	-	100,000
Retained Earnings	-	18,080
Total	**159,780**	**159,780**

CHAPTER 17

Applying What You've Learned to Accounting Ratios

Accounting ratios are another element of financial statement analysis. The accounting ratios are one of the reasons that principles like the revenue recognition principle, accrual accounting principle, matching principle, consistency principle, and others are so important. Without these principles, it would be impossible to interpret a financial statement in a way that makes it easier to use. Ratios can determine a company's liquidity, the number of assets to liabilities, and other important percentages. By breaking down ratios using a percent, it is easier to compare numbers across different accounting periods and notice trends in business.

Ratios are often referred to as financial ratios because they are designed to tell more about the financial aspect of a company.

You can express the ratio as a percentage by multiplying the resulting decimal by 100%. Below, you'll find a list of different types of ratios and a short summary of what each ratio tells you about the performance of a company. When an equation calls for an average, you'll take the amount listed on the balance sheet and the amount listed on the income statement. Add the two numbers and divide by two to arrive at the average.

Profitability Ratios

Gross Profit Rate = Gross Profit/Net Sales

This ratio describes the amount of total profit that has been generated from sales revenue. To arrive at a gross profit (a number that is not found on the balance sheet), you'll subtract any returns, discounts, or allowances from total sales. Then, you'll subtract the cost of sales to arrive at gross profit. This number is divided by net sales to arrive at the gross profit rate.

Return on Assets = Net Income/Average Total Assets

The return on assets is considered the return on assets. Essentially, this ratio evaluates how efficiently management is using their available assets and resources to create income for the company.

Return on Sales = Net Income/Net Sales

This ratio is also called the 'net profit rate' or the 'net profit margin'. It analyzes how much income is derived from dollar sales. As dollar sales are more reliable than accounts payable, a higher percentage here is preferred.

Return on Stockholders' Equity = Net Income/Average Stockholders' Equity

This calculates the amount of income that comes per dollar of owner's equity. In a way, this is a measure of how well owners are allocating stockholders' equity to turn a profit and give a greater return.

Liquidity Ratios

Cash Ratio = (Cash + Marketable Securities)/Current Liabilities

The cash ratio evaluates a company's ability to pay current liabilities with available cash and marketable securities. Items like stocks and bonds that are easily transferable are examples of marketable securities, which are short-term assets that are as good as cash for paying off debts. In a way, this also calculates some risk, as a company that relies on loans and accounts payable to pay debts may have problems meeting their obligations in months when there is less incoming revenue.

Current Ratio = Current Assets/Current Liabilities

This liquidity ratio evaluates how likely a company is to use current assets for their short-term obligations. The current assets include current receivables, prepayments, inventory, and marketable securities, in addition to available cash.

Net Working Capital = Current Assets – Current Liabilities

This ratio helps determine a company's ability to meet current liabilities. If the result is a positive number, then the company can meet its current liabilities using current assets. If there is a deficiency, the result will be displayed as a negative number.

Acid Test Ratio = Current Assets/Current Liabilities

This test is also known as the 'quick ratio'. The acid test is an analysis of a company's ability to pay short-term liabilities with short-term assets. Basically, it is a ratio measuring the current financial status without considering long-term statement items or equity.

Valuation and Growth Ratios

Earnings per Share = (Net Income – Preferred Dividends)/Average Common Shares Outstanding

This ratio shows the average rate of earnings for each share of common stock. Because this focuses only on common stock outstanding, the amount for preferred dividends is subtracted from net income.

Book Value per Share = Common Shareholders' Equity/Average Common Shares

By calculating the book value of each share, shareholders know if they have made a good investment. This ratio analyzes stock value compared to historical cost. The number of shares effects the payout for each share, so the number of shares that a company chooses to issue affects the overall value for each share. For example, if a company has $1,000 to distribute and has only issued 100 shares, each person would get $10 while the issuance of $1,000 to a group of 10,000 shares would leave each person with ten cents.

Price-Earnings Ratio = Market Price per Share/Earnings per Share

The price-earnings ratio helps determine if a stock is being sold at fair value, or if it is over- or under-priced. A lower ratio means the company is under-priced, while a higher ratio leads investors to expect a company to take their available earnings and use it to rapidly grow their business.

Dividend Yield Ratio = Dividend per Share/Market Price per Share

This ratio measures the return on dividends compared to how much each stock was purchased for. Usually, a higher ratio is appealing to investors that are interested in dividend payouts, rather than those looking at a company's long-term capital and assets.

Dividend Pay-Out Ratio = Dividend per Share/Earnings per Share

Even when a company has earnings leftover from a period, they often plan ahead to use some of it for expenses due next period rather than distribute it all as dividends. The pay-out ratio determines what percentage of dividends a company is paying out to owners and stockholders.

Leverage Ratios

Debt-Equity Ratio = Total Liabilities/Total Equity

This ratio helps determine the capital structure of a company in regard to how much of their debt comes liabilities compared to equity. If the ratio is greater than one, the company has leveraged many resources into their company, while a ratio of less than one signifies a company that is more conservative in their actions.

Debt Ratio = Total Liabilities/Total Assets

This ratio determines how much of a company's assets are financed by their debts and obligations to parties outside of the company. By subtracting the equity ratio from 1, you can also arrive at the debt ratio.

Equity Ratio = Total Equity/Total Assets

This ratio determines the percentage of assets a company has accumulated from equity from owners and stockholders in the company. By subtracting the debt ratio from 1, you can also arrive at the equity ratio.

Times Earned Interest = Earnings Before Interest (and Taxes)/ Interest Expense

This ratio calculates the interest a company earns on payments and loans. It measures how often interest is converted to income and the ability of the company to pay interest expense using profits from their earnings.

Management Efficiency Ratios

Receivable Turnover = Net Credit Sales/Average Accounts Receivable

This analyzes a company's ability to collect credit and due accounts. In a way, it measures how efficient it is for the company to offer credit terms to its customers and helps management decide how often they should collect on open accounts.

Inventory Turnover = Cost of Sales/Average Inventory

The inventory turnover rate indicates how often inventory is sold and replaced. Higher ratios show higher efficiency, as it indicates they are managing their inventory well. Some people may use total sales rather than the cost of sales to calculate this equation. The more accurate representation depends on the valuation of inventory and if it is listed at historical cost or market value.

Days Sales Outstanding = 365 Days/Receivable Turnover

This ratio may also be called 'collection period' or 'receivable turnover in days'. It determines the average days that it takes a company to collect on their accounts receivable. A lower number indicates better efficiency and fewer days that sales remain outstanding. Some accounts choose to use 360 days for this equation instead of 365.

Days Inventory Outstanding = 365 Days/Inventory Turnover

This ratio may also be called 'inventory turnover in days'. The resulting number is the days that inventory remains in the warehouse, tracking the period from the purchase of inventory to the sale of the same batch of inventory. A shorter turnover period is better.

Operating Cycle = Days Inventory Outstanding + Days Sales Outstanding

A complete operating cycle is described as purchasing merchandise, selling the products, then collecting any remaining due amounts. The entire number of days this takes is considered a full operating cycle. Shorter operating cycles mean that a company can quickly turnover inventory and collect on the remaining accounts, which means they accrue revenue faster.

Accounts Payable Turnover = Net Credit Purchases/Average Accounts Payable

This number represents how many times the accounts payable are paid in the average accounting period. Lower ratios are preferred, as it means a company is putting off their payable accounts temporarily and using the money in a more productive way. While paying a debt obligation early takes care of it, paying early also limits the availability of money for productive purposes in the business.

Days Payable Outstanding = 365 Days/Accounts Payable Turnover

This may also be considered the 'payment period' or 'accounts payable turnover in days'. Unlike inventory and sales, longer days payable outstanding is better because of the way it allows a company to better allocate their cash in a way that will generate profit.

Total Asset Turnover = Net Sales/Total Assets

This ratio measures how efficiently a company can use its assets to generate sales. This ratio is similar to that for return on assets, however, this ratio uses a company's net sales instead of their net income to generate the ratio.

Cash Conversion Cycle = Operating Cycle – Days Payable Outstanding

The cash conversion cycle describes how quickly a company can turn its cash generated in the operating cycle into more cash. It describes the payment for goods and materials, selling those goods, and then collecting any due amounts. A shorter cash conversion cycle is preferred.

Conclusion

Accounting principles are a carefully designed framework that allows companies and accountants some flexibility in choosing the methods that work best for them, while still creating a statement cohesive enough that it allows financial statements to be compared against other periods and the statements of other companies. This is especially important for publicly-traded companies, as their statements are subject to rigorous evaluation by a third-party certified public accountant that works outside of the company.

Hopefully, this book has been successful in breaking down everything you need to know to use accounting principles at work or in your day-to-day life. You should now be able to fully understand and analyze accounting statements, as well as use the information you've learned to put together balance sheets and calculate amounts like net worth, whether for your business or your personal earnings. This will help you easily track financial changes, understand ratios, and be sure that you can trust the data you are looking at for help making important decisions.

The next logical step is to start practicing. There are many rules that govern the field of accounting, so it may take some time before you master them all. Fortunately, this book should serve as a guideline that you can refer to as needed for clarity. With practice, you'll be able to confidently use these accounting principles as needed, at work and at home, to create, analyze, and understand financial statements.

Thank you again for downloading and good luck!

References

http://www.businessdictionary.com/definition/monetary-unit-principle.html

http://www.investorguide.com/article/13789/list-of-key-accounting-terms-and-definitions/

https://accounting-simplified.com/financial/statements/statement-of-financial-position.html

https://accounting-simplified.com/financial/statements/statement-of-changes-in-equity.html

https://accounting-simplified.com/financial/statements/types.html

https://business-accounting-guides.com/closing-entries/

https://cantorcriminallawyers.com/top-5-embezzlement-cases-in-america

https://corporatefinanceinstitute.com/resources/knowledge/accounting/t-accounts/

https://corporatefinanceinstitute.com/resources/knowledge/accounting/accrual-principle/

https://corporatefinanceinstitute.com/resources/knowledge/accounting/3-financial-statements-linked/

https://corporatefinanceinstitute.com/resources/knowledge/accounting/journal-entries-guide/

https://corporatefinanceinstitute.com/resources/knowledge/accounting/adjusting-entries/

https://corporatefinanceinstitute.com/resources/knowledge/accounting/matching-principle/

https://courses.lumenlearning.com/sac-finaccounting/chapter/journalizing-and-posting-closing-entries/

https://debitoor.com/dictionary/economic-entity-principle

https://debitoor.com/dictionary/materiality-principle

https://debitoor.com/dictionary/monetary-unit-principle

https://debitoor.com/dictionary/time-period-principle

https://pakaccountants.com/courses/statement-of-comprehensive-income-statement/

https://smallbusiness.chron.com/example-cashbasis-accounting-30568.html

https://www.accountingcoach.com/balance-sheet/explanation

https://www.accountingcoach.com/balance-sheet/explanation/2

https://www.accountingcoach.com/balance-sheet/explanation/3

https://www.accountingcoach.com/balance-sheet/explanation/4

https://www.accountingcoach.com/blog/what-are-accounting-ratios

https://www.accountingcoach.com/blog/what-is-the-cost-principle

https://www.accountingcoach.com/blog/what-is-the-difference-between-a-nominal-account-and-a-real-account

https://www.accountingcoach.com/blog/what-is-the-full-disclosure-principle

https://www.accountingcoach.com/blog/what-is-the-matching-principle

https://www.accountingcoach.com/debits-and-credits/explanation

References

https://www.accountingformanagement.org/business-entity-concept/

https://www.accountingformanagement.org/consistency-principle-of-accounting/

https://www.accountingformanagement.org/full-disclosure-principle/

https://www.accountingformanagement.org/going-concern-concept/

https://www.accountingtools.com/articles/2017/5/14/the-conservatism-principle

https://www.accountingtools.com/articles/2017/5/14/the-cost-principle

https://www.accountingtools.com/articles/2017/5/14/the-economic-entity-principle

https://www.accountingtools.com/articles/2017/5/14/the-full-disclosure-principle

https://www.accountingtools.com/articles/2017/5/14/the-going-concern-principle

https://www.accountingtools.com/articles/2017/5/14/the-matching-principle

https://www.accountingtools.com/articles/2017/5/14/the-materiality-principle

https://www.accountingtools.com/articles/2017/5/15/basic-accounting-principles

https://www.accountingtools.com/articles/2017/5/15/percentage-of-completion-method

https://www.accountingtools.com/articles/2017/5/15/reliability-principle

https://www.accountingtools.com/articles/2017/5/15/the-accrual-principle

https://www.accountingtools.com/articles/2017/5/15/the-cash-method-of-accounting

https://www.accountingtools.com/articles/2017/5/15/the-consistency-principle

https://www.accountingtools.com/articles/2017/5/15/the-monetary-unit-principle

https://www.accountingtools.com/articles/2017/5/15/the-revenue-recognition-principle

https://www.accountingtools.com/articles/2017/5/15/the-time-period-principle

https://www.accountingtools.com/articles/2018/1/27/reserve

https://www.accountingtools.com/articles/what-is-a-cash-basis-income-statement.html

https://www.accountingverse.com/accounting-basics/accounting-cycle.html

https://www.accountingverse.com/accounting-basics/elements-of-accounting.html

https://www.accountingverse.com/accounting-basics/financial-statements-introduction.html

https://www.accountingverse.com/accounting-basics/statement-of-owners-equity.html

https://www.accountingverse.com/accounting-basics/statement-of-owners-equity.html

https://www.accountingverse.com/managerial-accounting/fs-analysis/financial-ratios.html

References

https://www.dummies.com/business/accounting/ten-common-notes-to-the-financial-statements/

https://www.fasb.org/jsp/FASB/Document_C/DocumentPage?cid=1176171746896&acceptedDisclaimer=true

https://www.fasb.org/jsp/FASB/Page/SectionPage&cid=1176171747007

https://www.fool.com/investing/2019/07/01/a-foolish-take-nearly-everythings-winning-in-2019.aspx

https://www.investopedia.com/ask/answers/030415/what-are-differences-between-deferred-expenses-and-prepaid-expenses.asp

https://www.investopedia.com/ask/answers/030415/what-are-differences-between-deferred-expenses-and-prepaid-expenses.asp

https://www.investopedia.com/ask/answers/06/amortizationvsdepreciation.asp

https://www.investopedia.com/ask/answers/06/rulesandpriciplesbasedaccounting.asp

https://www.investopedia.com/terms/a/accountingmethod.asp

https://www.myaccountingcourse.com/accounting-cycle/journal-entries

https://www.myaccountingcourse.com/accounting-dictionary/cost-principle

https://www.myaccountingcourse.com/accounting-dictionary/economic-entity-assumption

https://www.myaccountingcourse.com/accounting-dictionary/monetary-unit-assumption

https://www.myaccountingcourse.com/accounting-principles/full-disclosure-principle

https://www.myaccountingcourse.com/accounting-principles/going-concern-concept

https://www.myaccountingcourse.com/accounting-principles/materiality-concept

https://www.rasmussen.edu/degrees/business/blog/basic-accounting-terms-acronyms-and-abbreviations-students-should/

https://www.thebalancesmb.com/how-to-prepare-a-statement-of-cash-flows-393584

https://www.wallstreetmojo.com/liquid-assets/

https://www.wikihow.com/Calculate-Depreciation-on-Fixed-Assets

https://xplaind.com/148829/cash-flow-statement

https://xplaind.com/257099/matching

https://xplaind.com/519095/post-closing-trial-balance

https://xplaind.com/605604/time-period

https://xplaind.com/668836/unadjusted-trial-balance

https://xplaind.com/936886/materiality

Made in the USA
Middletown, DE
07 December 2021